The Purposeful Child

A Quick and Practical Parenting Guide to Creating the
Optimal Home Environment for Young Children

Lorena T. Seidel, M.Ed.

Archway Publishing books may be ordered through booksellers or by contacting:

Archway Publishing
1663 Liberty Drive
Bloomington, IN 47403
www.archwaypublishing.com
1 (888) 242-5904

Because of the dynamic nature of the Internet, any web addresses or links contained in this book may have changed since publication and may no longer be valid. The views expressed in this work are solely those of the author and do not necessarily reflect the views of the publisher, and the publisher hereby disclaims any responsibility for them.

Any people depicted in stock imagery provided by Thinkstock are models, and such images are being used for illustrative purposes only. Certain stock imagery © Thinkstock.

ISBN: 978-1-4808-1563-6 (sc)
ISBN: 978-1-4808-1564-3 (e)

Print information available on the last page.

Archway Publishing rev. date: 10/30/2015

To my sweet daughters; Annabelle, baby Julliette, and Pollyanna.

Contents

Preface

The most important part of life is not the age of university studies, but the first one, the period from birth to the age of six. For that is the time when a man's intelligence itself, his greatest implement, is being formed.
—Dr. Maria Montessori

Before I became a mother, I was a Montessori teacher. I received my certification from the American Montessori Society (AMS), and I was fortunate to teach at Whitby School, located in Greenwich, Connecticut. Whitby School is the first American Montessori school in the country, and it has offered me an opportunity to learn from the most excellent educators.

In the classroom, I witnessed toddlers, preschoolers, and kindergarteners thriving as they developed valuable life skills through performing meaningful everyday tasks. These were simple tasks such as slicing bananas, serving themselves snacks, putting their shoes and coats on, cleaning up their messes, or arranging flowers in vases to be placed around the room. They performed these activities by themselves with little to no help from the teachers or any other adults. They also solved conflicts with one another peacefully and respectfully (with the guidance of adults), and there was mutual respect among teachers and students. This thriving environment—not only physical, but emotional—is inspiring for those young children and fostered their sense of purpose.

While awaiting the birth of my first child, I transformed my home and created an environment based on the principles I had studied and used as a teacher. One mom and dad, who were parents of a student in my classroom, told me all about bringing Montessori into the home. They had really embraced it as a lifestyle and a valuable parenting tool. They told me that in their home they did not use praise, rewards, or punishments to manage behavior or to attempt to win cooperation. Their children slept on low beds, fed themselves at a small table using real utensils, and were even potty trained by seventeen months. I was impressed. Like any other expectant mom, I had to learn all about this magical way of raising a young child, which was different from everything I knew about parenting.

I was fascinated, excited, and inspired. I started to prepare my home environment while keeping the child's perspective in mind, and it became addictive. Finding new ways to make the world accessible to my daughter fed my creativity. After witnessing firsthand how much my toddler could do for herself, I knew I needed to share the idea with others.

I had gone to many playgroups and watched young children playing in environments that were fully child-proofed with gates, latches, outlet covers, foam corners, and more. However, we moms still spent too much time and energy saying the word *no*, chasing our babies around, and making sure they were not getting into things or getting hurt. This interrupted the child's play, exploration, and concentration. For sure, mothers of young children should be concerned about safety and should supervise their children. But when a *prepared space,* and not simply a *childproofed space,* is in place, it provides safety while meeting the needs of the child and diminishing the constant parental intervention and overprotection.

I realized the home environment I had created was beneficial both to my children and to me. It made our lives easier. It was a "yes" kind of home. Yes, you can open the cabinet below the sink. The chemicals are no longer there. Yes, you can help me unload the dishwasher. Plates and glasses are stored at your level. Yes, you can wipe your face by yourself. There is an unbreakable mirror and a cloth within your reach. Yes, you can crawl around and play until you are ready to sleep. The entire bedroom works as a safe playpen, and the bed is low. Yes, you can make your own snack. Things are sized for a child and are safe and accessible. This realization was what prompted me to create an interactive e-book called *Everyday Montessori* and later the parenting DVD series, *The Purposeful Child*.

The idea was so simple. I could not believe more people were not doing it. In my quest to give my children more purposeful days and make the world more accessible to them, I minimized the clutter, made my own cleaning products, and became healthier. In my quest to break bad parenting habits and approach discipline in a more positive way, my husband and I became more nonpunitive, nonpermissive, respectful, and intentional parents.

During this period of my life, I was also completing my master's degree in elementary education at Sacred Heart University. As I delved into the field of education, I confirmed what I already knew: there was a great need for parent education. I made this the focus of my thesis.

My thesis research project presented a parent and child educational program. This project consisted of six workshops. Each class was an opportunity for parents to learn how to apply research-based educational strategies and activities at home. While parents learned, children explored a prepared learning environment and interacted with others. Parents were introduced to techniques on creating the optimal physical and psychological home environment for young children.

The goal was to empower parents with new disciplinary and educational tools to ultimately improve children's independence, concentration, language, self-confidence, and other valuable social-emotional and life skills. I implemented this educational program in the fall of 2012 for a period of six weeks and repeated it in the winter, spring, and summer sessions of 2013. Parents' feedback was so positive that I elaborated upon my research and experience in creating this book.

After my second child, I had left the classroom and started to consult with families to help create these optimum home environments for their children. I was passionate about children and enjoyed working with them in the classroom. However, I felt I was more effective and could have a greater impact on children's lives when educating their parents instead. I could help children for a few hours, or I could work with their parents who would then bring the valuable principles and concepts continuously into their children's lives.

With this book, I suggest a reformed approach to parenting. Brain research from the past couple of decades has given us a better idea of how children develop and learn. Before then, humans had been parenting based on intuition, cultural and evolutionary needs, and parenting tales passed down from generation to generation.

Now, we have the chance to parent more efficiently and effectively. Much is heard about the need for educational reform that will accommodate the quickly changing world and prepare our children for twenty-first-century lifestyles. However, I believe there is an even greater need for a different kind of reform—reform toward purposeful parenting.

Using my experience as an educator and a mother of three, I combined the most effective practices in order to help parents create more peaceful, positive, and purposeful homes.

I live with my husband, Andrew, and our three daughters, Pollyanna, Annabelle, and Julliette, in Rowayton, CT. The children explore our prepared environment, perform everyday tasks, and learn by doing. Peaceful songs, bread making, mint tea, storytelling, nature walks, building blocks, and typical challenging behaviors fill our days. I continue to learn and teach about parenting professionally. However, I am still in the beginning of my parenting journey, and the work I do is mainly for me because I do need the constant reminders and the practice that purposeful parenting requires.

The Purposeful Child is a guide to creating the optimal home environment for young children. This is a brief and clear (short and sweet) booklet in which I summarized my researched and hard earned lessons in the most succinct manner to allow busy parents to gain as much value in the least amount of time. The principles and concepts in this book can be used to help children of all ages. However, this book focus on parents of young children (toddlers- kindergarten).

It draws upon research from approaches renowned for their proven success. These include the work of parent educator and psychologist Haim G. Ginott; Adlerian psychology and principles that Alfred Adler developed and Rudolf Dreikurs further advanced; and the teachings of positive discipline elaborated by Jane Nelsen and Lynn Lot inspired by the work of Adler and Dreikurs. I also draw upon research from progressive methods of education, such as the Montessori method, developed by Dr. Maria Montessori; Waldorf education, developed by philosopher Rudolf Steiner; and the latest brain research.

The home is the child's first learning environment. However, young children are living in busy spaces made for adults. Our physical home environments can be transformed to avoid frustration and to inspire children to perform everyday tasks independently or with little help. Young children benefit from functioning easily and accomplishing things on their own without feeling overwhelmed or overstimulated.

Parents are a child's first and most influential teachers. Yet most of us have little to no training when it comes to parenting. The way we handle ordinary issues with our children—tantrums, power struggles, playground conflicts, and such—will impact who our children will be as adults.

How can we raise a purposeful child? How can we provide more meaningful days to our young children?

Parents want to raise independent, resilient, responsible, capable, and emotionally stable children. Simple transformations in both the child's physical and emotional environments can help develop those valuable social, emotional, and life skills. Long-term, nonpunitive, nonpermissive, respectful, constructive, encouraging, and loving parenting methods fill this book. *The Purposeful Child* goal is to help parents bring more joy, peace, and purpose into their children's lives.

Introduction

I often start a parenting workshop by saying, "Anyone here who is not having any trouble parenting, please raise your hand." Everyone laughs, and of course no one ever raises his or her hand. Parenting is hard.

I continue the workshop by brainstorming two lists with the attendees. First, parents share the problems and concerns they currently have with their young children. This list incorporates issues such as whining, power struggles, back talk, hitting, morning or bedtime hassles, tantrums, sibling rivalry, difficulty sharing, and other poor behaviors. While one person shouts his or her concern, most other parents nod in agreement.

After brainstorming this first list, I tell parents to close their eyes, fast-forward in time, and imagine their children at twenty-five. They are coming home for Thanksgiving dinner. I ask, "What characteristics would you like your grown child to have? How would you like him or her to be?" I create another list from their answers. They would like their grown children to be responsible, kind, resilient, capable, confident, independent, happy, passionate, honest, creative, and more.

We look at both lists side by side.

Parenting Challenges (Today)	Desired Characteristics of Children (Future)
Whining	Responsible
Power struggles	Kind
Back talk	Resilient
Hitting	Capable
Morning or bedtime hassle	Confident
Tantrums	Independent
Sibling rivalry	Creative
Problems sharing	Passionate
Toilet training	Honest
More	More

The list of challenges is where the group is right now, and the second list is where the group wants to get. We must work toward all those wonderful life skills that make up the second list. This second list is the big picture—the goal. Those parents have learned to embrace the challenges with a positive state of mind. Knowing that who our children become as adults is directly impacted by the way we handle every issue we have with them today. Next time your child is having a tantrum, a power struggle, or a playground conflict, see it as a unique chance to teach him or her valuable social-emotional and life skills.

Parents desire to be the best they can. Even before the birth of a child, parents begin their quest to provide their child with the best chances for success. Even after consulting much material about how best to parent, many are left hopeless. Learning begins at birth and continues throughout life. However, a child's early developmental period is the most crucial. In the first seven years of life, a child undergoes striking physical and psychological development. The foundation is laid for all future development, and it is arguably the most important time for both fostering a love of learning and allowing children to reach their potential. Parents are their child's first and most influential teachers.

They have the greatest impact on the child's social, emotional, and academic success. It is logical, therefore, that parents take full advantage of this unique period to help children reach their utmost potential.

Parents are the master planners of the child's surroundings, schedule, and activities. Even so, many parents lack effective tools to raise an independent, resilient, responsible, capable, and emotionally stable child. Are we teaching our children to manage their time and help themselves, or are we controlling every aspect of our child's life? Are we fostering their independence, or are we doing for them what they can already do for themselves? Are we encouraging them to solve conflicts, or are we constantly intervening and refereeing?

Young children want to do things for themselves, and they like to help. When simple items needed to perform everyday tasks independently are not accessible, when we decline their help, and when we insist on doing things for them and go around fixing their attempts, children often stop collaborating with parents. They start to act helpless and feel frustrated and discouraged. When children feel discouraged, they misbehave. When children misbehave, parents often try to regain collaboration. They try to turn bad behavior around by using some of the most common parenting tools:

- Yelling
- Blaming
- Shaming
- Rewarding
- Praising
- Threatening
- Bribing
- Nagging
- Utilizing time-outs

We don't want the two-year-old to help clear the table because we don't want him or her to break the plate. We save the dish but break the child's courage and confidence. A child puts on his or her shoes, and we say, "That shoe is on the wrong foot, sweetie." When the child attempts to help, we say, "Let me make the bed, honey. Those covers are too heavy for you." When children fight over a toy, we take it away. We also often take away the chance to learn about conflict resolution. Children receive the message that they are

- small,
- not good enough,
- incapable,
- inadequate,
- unimportant, or
- inferior.

We obliviously continue to demonstrate our superiority and our child's inferiority day after day. Lacking faith in the child's ability, courage, and adequacy robs his or her sense of security and hinders the development of self-sufficiency. Are we taking away our child's sense of purpose?

To achieve our lifelong parenting goals, we need to use everyday challenges as opportunities to teach valuable life skills to our children. Remember the list of challenges and desired characteristics of children? That is our road map.

Modern research from many philosophers, educators, psychologists, occupational therapists, and brain specialists states that in order to acquire valuable life skills, children need to experience the following:

- Hands-on and multisensory play
- Collaboration instead of competition
- Respect for their interests and learning pace
- Meaningful learning rather than passively receiving information
- Freedom to be themselves and make acceptable choices
- Prepared environments that meet their needs and interests
- Guidance focused on their strengths and not on their deficits

Those principles permeate this guide at multiple levels. Providing our children with those experiences might require us to change our expectations of young children, our home environment, and ourselves. There are three key components to helping develop a purposeful child: the child, the environment, and the adult.

The Child

*We discovered that education is not something which the teacher does, but that it is
a natural process which develops spontaneously in the human being.*
—Dr. Maria Montessori

Children develop through a natural process. For centuries adults have mistakenly approached young children convinced they know exactly how to teach and what to pour into children's minds. However, research now shows that children's own curiosity guides them to learn and explore. The child's sophisticated neurological network is built as the child engages with the environment and physically explores his or her surroundings. Tremendous development will not happen unless the child engages in purposeful and experimental interactions with the environment and the adults around him or her (especially the parents).

The Environment

*We learn to do something by doing it.
There is no other way.*
—John Holt

An intentionally prepared environment can develop feelings in a child of being capable, confident, and competent. Young children show interest in real-life activities by pretending to cook, clean, take care of a doll, or carry out adult conversations. But children would much rather do real things. Any daily activity such as washing fruits and vegetables, setting or clearing a table, watering plants, sorting laundry, sweeping, or helping in the garden helps children take real responsibility in the home and feel purposeful. Children who are allowed to practice everyday

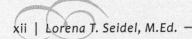

activities for themselves are developing important skills such as attention, concentration, planning, organization, problem solving, collaboration, and self-confidence.

The Adult

Don't worry that children never listen to you; worry that they are always watching you.
—Robert Fulghum

Adults set the social-emotional climate in the home. We are responsible for what comes into our homes, how we arrange our environment, how we interact with each other, and how we behave in front of our children. Both the physical and emotional environments are important. We parents have the biggest job. We help our children grow up to feel a sense of belonging and significance, and we teach life and social skills.

A predictable daily rhythm, limited screen time (including television, computer, video games, phones, and more), a positive approach to discipline, and healthy social interactions are critical in the development of a young child. A positive home atmosphere also fosters confidence, independence, and a strong sense of purpose.

Therefore, your child, your home, and you create a learning triangle. The environment is a home specially prepared and designed to aid in learning. The adult is the role model, guide, and nurturer who provides the link between the environment and the child. The child uses the adult's guidance and experiential interactions with the environment to build knowledge and develop at his or her own pace.

Part I—The Child

Reasons Children Do What They Do and What They Need to Thrive

Before attempting to correct misbehaviors, parents must understand why they happen in the first place. Whining, tantrums, power struggles, and back talk are the symptoms of a deeper issue. Children are reaching out for help. They are not trying to misbehave.

Often adults have unrealistic expectations of their young child. What looks like misbehavior is frequently developmentally appropriate. Young children need to climb onto things, run around, and touch things to learn how the world works. They need to cry and have temper tantrums to release and process their emotions. Young children need to test parents and push buttons to learn about boundaries.

The first thing parents need to check is if the child's basic needs are being met. Some of those basic needs are these:

- To sleep
- To eat
- To feel healthy
- To experiment
- To move
- To explore

- To be social
- To be challenged
- To be stimulated
- To feel loved
- To feel independent

Meeting most of those needs is the responsibility of the adults. Our job as parents is to meet the child's needs. In the process, young children will learn how to meet their own needs as they grow. Ask yourself if you are trying to run one too many errands, if you are pushing nap time too late, or if you are shopping for dinner at 5:00 p.m. when everyone is tired and hungry. Parents can push children over the edge. Often when a toddler is having a temper tantrum in the store, the parent is the one at fault.

Next, parents must be sure the poor behavior is not simply due to lack of a specific skill. For example, a three year old who is showing aggressive behavior (biting, hitting, pushing, and more) could be simply lacking verbal/communication skills. Children must be taught or reminded about those skills. You must consistently demonstrate the skill before you can expect your child to use it. For example, you will have to teach, demonstrate, role-play, and model conflict resolution several times before you can expect your young child to successfully navigate the ins and outs of win-win negotiation.

A child's behavior has a purpose. It is important for parents to have a good understanding of child development in order to establish realistic expectations about the child's behavior. So what do children need to thrive? Most importantly, children need *belonging* and *significance*. Many other things will contribute to the formation of personality. This includes role models; family dynamic; family rhythm; the child's perception of self, others, and the world; and a prepared environment.

The Need for Love and Power

Man does not see reality as it is, but only as he perceives it, and his perception may be mistaken or biased.
—Rudolf Dreikurs

Parents often ask me: *How do I handle my two-year-old who has become very clingy and is whining and testing boundaries lately? I am so annoyed and angry. I don't know what to do.*

Children, like all humans, are goal oriented. A child's primary goal is to feel a sense of belonging and significance. That is just how we human beings are wired. A sense of belonging relates to the need for unconditional love, emotional connection, and positive attention. A sense of significance relates to the need for personal power, autonomy, and the ability to make meaningful contributions. Without meeting both of these innate needs (love and power), children will not develop to their full potential.

Children's bad behaviors are attempts to feel this sense of love and power we all need. However, children act in ineffective ways because they have developed what Adlerian psychology refers as *a mistaken purpose*. Children always have reasons behind their behavior. However, many times the child's reasons and goals are misguided.

When children don't feel they are being loved, they will usually try something negative to get the love back (attention-seeking behaviors such as whining, clinging, or acting helpless). When children are feeling out of control and powerless, they might try something negative to get the power back (fighting back with power-seeking behaviors such as throwing tantrums, talking back, not listening, and more). Bad behavior is not the actual problem. It's just a symptom of a deeper issue. Parents need to address the root causes of misbehavior. That way, children will get what they need in a more positive way.

In his book *Children: The Challenge*, Rudolf Dreikurs states that four main mistaken purposes might motivate children's actions. They are *attention*, *power*, *revenge*, and *inadequacy*.

It is important that parents first determine that misbehavior is not simply age, skill, or developmentally appropriate, or due to lack of a special skill. If the bad behavior does not seem to follow unfulfilled basic needs or lack of skills, then the child's need for love and power or feelings of revenge and inadequacy could be motivating the child's behavior. Children behave with purpose. Until parents understand the purpose of the child's misbehavior, they can't be sure how to redirect that child. One way for you to understand your child's goal is to determine how he or she is inviting you to feel.

Generally, when the adult describes feeling annoyed by a child's bad behavior, the child is usually using attention-seeking behavior. The behavior is annoying, but the message is, "Notice me. Involve me usefully."

Usually when the adult describes feeling anger or frustration, those are signs that the child is making a misguided attempt for power. The child's behavior might seem defiant, but the coded message is, "Let me help. Give me choices."

The next time your child's behavior makes you annoyed, guilty, or frustrated, take a deep breath. Imagine he or she is saying, "I want to belong and feel significant, but I don't know how to do it. I am using these annoying, attention-seeking tactics and engaging you in endless power struggles because I don't know what else to do."

Why Children Misbehave

Seeking Attention

Does your child's behavior invite you to feel annoyed or irritated? When you reprimand your child or give your child attention, does he or she temporarily stop the disturbing action but later repeat the bad behavior? Is your child displaying attention-seeking behaviors such as whining, clinging, acting helpless, or even fighting with siblings? Then your child's mistaken goal could be attention.

Perhaps you have been too busy with work or brought home a new baby. Perhaps you are simply taking a phone call. The child's actions are annoying, but they say, "I am loved only when I am being noticed or being served. I want to belong." In that moment the child believes he or she is lacking that sense of unconditional love.

The child who is seeking attention needs one of these actions by the parent:

- To be noticed, involved, or redirected by feeling useful in a meaningful task.
- To know he or she can rely on a special time alone with you later. The adult could say, "I love you, and I am looking forward to our special time together this afternoon."
- To be taught better ways to ask for love and attention. The child could be redirected to say, "Mom, I need love," "Give me a hug," or "I want you to play a game with me."
- A consistent and kind and firm response from you.
- A consistent family rhythm and routine.
- To be touched and validated without shame, blame, or lectures. (This is touch without saying anything.)

Seeking Power

Does your child's behavior invite you to feel provoked, challenged, or angry? Does it make you feel you need to prove your power with phrases such as "I will make you do it" or "You cannot get away with this"? When your child is reprimanded, does he or she intensify the action? Does he or she want to win, be the boss, and fight back? Is your child displaying power struggles such as tantrums, fighting, back talk, and more? Then your child's mistaken goal could be power.

Perhaps he or she feels stripped of power because you are doing things for your child he or she is capable of doing alone. Perhaps you are constantly overprotecting, directing, correcting, and making all the decisions—robbing your child of a sense of free will, independence, and some control over his or her life. The child is saying, "Engage me in something purposeful. Stop bossing me around. Let me help, and give me choices." Your child believes he or she lacks a sense of personal power, independence, and autonomy.

A child who is engaging you in power struggles needs one of these actions by the parent:

- To be invited to help.
- To feel validated. ("I cannot make you do it, and I need your help.")
- To be given limited and acceptable choices. ("You can put your pajamas on by yourself, or I can help you.")
- A kind but firm adult who decides what to do and follows through. (Say it once, and then act.)
- The routine or rhythm to become the boss—not you. (Create a routine chart with your child. Then you can say, "What is next on your routine chart?" instead of nagging, reminding, correcting, and directing.)
- An environment that promotes independence and encourages that child to perform tasks on his or her own with little to no help.

Seeking Revenge

Does your child's behavior invite you to feel hurt or disappointed? Do you ask yourself, "How could my child do this to me?" When you reprimand your child, does he or she want to get even, hurt you or others, or damage property? Does he or she make himself or herself unlikable? Then your child's mistaken goal could be revenge.

Perhaps you have hurt your child's feelings by spending too much time with the new baby, taking sides during sibling fights, or sending him or her to a time-out. To seek revenge, children might hit, slam the door, say, "I hate you," "You are mean," or "You cannot come to my birthday," and more. Your child's actions seem to be saying, "I want to hurt others because I feel hurt. I cannot be loved, and I will make you suffer." Your child believes he or she is not important, significant, or loved.

A child who is seeking revenge needs one of these actions by the parent:

- The adult to deal with the hurt feelings. You can say, "You must feel hurt. Can we talk about that?" or "I must have hurt your feelings. What can I do to help you feel better?"
- The adult to not take the child's actions personally.
- Reaffirmation of his or her worth.
- Encouragement.
- To feel loved and connected. (Connect before you correct or direct.)

Feeling Inadequate

Does your child's behavior invite you to feel despair, pity, and helplessness? When you reprimand the child, does he or she feel there is no use to try? Does he or she feel passive and withdrawn? Then your child's mistaken goal could be inadequacy.

You might have disparaged your child, set very high expectations, criticized his or her performance, or fixed something he or she did. When a child feels inadequate he or she might withdraw or say, "I cannot do it." The child is trying to say, "I cannot do anything right, so I will not even try. I am not good. I cannot do this as well as you do." The child believes he or she is not going to be satisfactory or will make a mistake and be judged.

A child who has been assumed to be inadequate needs the parent to take one of these actions:

- To take time for teaching or training.
- To be set up for small successes that will rebuild his or her self-confidence.
- To be trusted, and told you will not give up on him or her.
- To feel encouraged to build on his or her interests.

The mistaken goals are listed in order of difficulty to treat. If the child fails to achieve the amount of desired recognition, the child travels into the next stage. Children who do not have a sense of belonging attempt to gain attention from parents, teachers, siblings, and peers. When children are not satisfied with their attempts at gaining attention, they often seek power by refusing to do what adults ask. When children's attempts at seeking power fail, they might seek revenge through behaviors such as hurting, defacing property, saying hurtful things, and more. When all else fails, children might display inadequacy by withdrawing and giving up.

To get to the root of a child's bad behavior, we must check our emotional states. Understand what the child is trying to communicate and the reason behind the behavior. Then meet the unmet need by choosing a method and following through. Remember that bad behavior is your child communicating an unmet need. When your child feels understood, valued, and empowered in a mutually respectful way, there is less need to misbehave.

Children Need Worthy Role Models

Children repeat what they see others doing, and they mirror the actions of others. Scientists have discovered a set of neurons in the human brain called mirror neurons or "monkey see, monkey do" neurons. This explains why we sometimes yawn when someone yawns in front of us or why we might get emotional when the person next to us is emotional. It can also explain why laughing is contagious.

The most powerful parenting tool we have is our behavior. When we are educating or disciplining a child, modeling is far more effective than lecturing. Everything we *do* is much more important than what we *say*. We often do not pay attention to what we do and how our children might perceive it. We toss our car keys to our spouses, but when our children throw things around, we reprimand them. We might shut cabinet doors with our feet, but when our toddlers kick the furniture, it is unacceptable. Our children will imitate our ways of walking, moving, and talking. They will imitate our vocabulary, emotions, manners, respect and consideration (or lack thereof) for others, and more.

As parents we can take advantage of those mirror neurons and make everyday life easier. We can occasionally exaggerate some of our actions to catch children's attention and make a point. For example, brush your teeth as you hand your child his or her toothbrush. No words are needed. Look your child in the eyes and say, "Time to put on your shoes and jacket." Do so as you are already putting on your own shoes and jacket. Whisper when you want your child to lower his or her voice, or walk really slowly when you want him or her to stop running.

As with any other tactic, this might not work every time or with every child, but young children imitate what we do—good and bad. Therefore, be mindful and intentional with your actions. Always trying to bring love and care into all we do is essential. This will enable our children to foster those qualities within themselves and will make us models worthy of our children's imitation.

A Positive Family Dynamic

*Being in a family is like being in a play. Each birth order position is like a different part in
a play, with distinct and separate characteristics for each part. Therefore, if one sibling has
already filled a part, such as the good child, other siblings may feel they have to find other parts
to play, such as rebellious child, academic child, athletic child, social child, and so on.*

—Jane Nelson

The family dynamic impacts a child's behavior, self-image, and personality. For example, children are different depending on birth order or how parents treat each child. The addition of each child changes the dynamic of the whole family. The following is a quick, simple, and grossly generalized illustration of how children might feel in their families.

Only children usually experience a high sense of love since they are usually the centers of their parents' worlds. However, the only child might have a really high or really low sense of personal power (autonomy and independence), depending on the parent. A high sense of power occurs if the child is given responsibilities and autonomy. A low sense of power occurs if parents are very protective or do everything for the only child.

Firstborns usually have a high sense of love since they initially receive undivided love and attention. They usually also have a high sense of personal power since they are encouraged to be very capable, responsible leaders and role models to younger siblings.

With the addition of a baby, the firstborn sees the attention and love the baby gets and how adults respond to the baby's every need. The baby cries and gets attention, or the baby soils his or her diaper and gets attention. Therefore, the older child might regress to needier behavior such as whining, crying, backsliding on toilet training, and so on.

Middle children usually develop a low sense of love because they feel they must compete for love and attention from the start. They often also develop a low sense of personal power because parents or older siblings often do things for them. Middle children can feel inadequate as they perceive their older sibling to be stronger and more capable.

With the addition of a baby, the middle child might think the parents prefer the older child. After all, parents seek the older child's help with the new baby more often, and parents trust the older child to be more capable. The middle child also might think the parents prefer the youngest child because the middle child sees the love and attention the baby gets.

The youngest children generally feel a high sense of love because they are the babies, and they have the attention of parents and older siblings. (However, if the child is the youngest of four or five, things could be different. The youngest child may not be getting too much love and attention.) The youngest children often develop a low sense of power as parents and siblings do too much for them and are constantly entertaining or holding them. The youngest children might feel helpless, as if parents don't expect much of them. They might feel that their parents compare them to the more capable and better skilled older siblings and that parents overprotect them from siblings.

Children need to feel they are being treated the same, no matter the birth order. Parents would never consciously prefer one child over the other. But how a child perceives a situation is what matters. Often parents take sides during sibling rivalries, functioning as referees. This often creates bullies and victims in the home. Parents can allow children to fall into certain roles within the family. The oldest is the leader; the middle one is difficult; and the little one is always a baby. This is discouraging for all the children and can have a negative psychological impact. Children see themselves as they are labeled and subconsciously live up to that.

> *The danger of favoritism can hardly be stated too dramatically. Almost every discouragement*
> *in childhood springs from the feeling that someone else is preferred.*
> —Alfred Adler

Here is a question a mom asked me after one of my lectures: *I have a two-and-a-half-year-old son and a nine-month-old daughter. Recently he started pushing her over. She can sit up on her own now but is still young enough that sometimes she falls over herself. He will gently push her over until she falls and cries. How do you deal with your kids pushing/hitting? Aren't some situations deserving of a punishment?*

Punishment can be especially dangerous with sibling rivalry because it will invite the child to further resent the sibling. It will show that you are taking sides, and that will set them apart instead of strengthening their bound.

Here are some examples of simple tools I usually use:

- Supervision. I try to stay close and stop any aggression before it happens. (This is the hardest with three children, and I often fail.) I stop the pushing by gently blocking with my hands or by removing the baby/other child out of the way. I gently say, "I will not let you push/hurt/(other action)," or I use the validation of feelings, as mentioned next.

- Allow and validate the child's feelings. Say, "I can see the baby upsets you sometimes," or "Having a little sister can be hard."

- I would not take sides. Treat them the same. Avoid creating a bully and victim roles in your family. At the time, when I see the aggression, I say, "I can see the two of you are having a hard time playing together" (even if it seems silly to say it to the baby, but it shows I am treating them the same, and I am not taking sides). I might also say, "I will have to separate the two of you," and I take the baby to another room.

- Focus on the solution. I often go to the aggressor first and ask, "What can you do to help her feel better?" or "Let's get her some ice," or "Let's find her a toy she can play with," or "Maybe you can color her a picture," and help the "aggressor" to become part of the solution and not part of the problem. Let him try to fix the situation.

- Follow through. If one insists on hurting/pushing, you can decide what you will do and then follow through. Instead of using time-out, or punishing, I might say, "It looks like you are having a hard time not pushing children today, and I will have to keep you close to me." Then I will stand next to her and hold her hand, or I will pick her up and hold her, or I will bring her next to me while I cook dinner. I might add, "Let me know when you feel ready to try again without hurting."

- Sportscast the situation. Sometimes something happens while I am in another room and I hear crying. I come in and describe what I see: "I see two little girls playing. I see there is only one doll, and two girls wanting to play with it," or "I see Annabelle is crying and looks like she is hurt." This helps them see the situation more clearly and think of a solution.

- Channel the child's feeling toward a more appropriate and productive behavior. Offer a chance to let the feelings/energy out by giving the child a pillow to scratch/punch/push or a ball to kick, or an almond to bite on, for example. I also give them some other alternatives to aggression such as walking away or asking me for help.

- Stop being the referee. Depending on the situation with my older girls, I might come in and say, "I trust you can figure this out on your own," or "Do you need my help solving this problem?" or "I cannot make you stop fighting, and I need your help," or "It looks like you need some time away from each other."

Other general principles that have helped me prevent sibling rivalry include encouraging cooperation, not competition; avoiding comparing children; not making a fuss over the baby in front of my older child; making sure every child gets special one-on-one time alone with my husband and with me.

Constructive Perceptions About Self, Others, and the World

Our purpose is not to set forth a series of techniques to manipulate behavior so that children always respond. Our purpose is to speak to what is best in our children—their intelligence, their initiative, their sense of responsibility, their sense of humor, their ability to be sensitive to the needs of others. We want to put an end to talk that wounds the spirit and search out the language that nourishes self-esteem.
—Adele Faber and Elaine Mazlish

What children think and how they feel about themselves, others, and the world around them influence their ability to learn new concepts, manage their behaviors, and relate to others. Young children are always making decisions about themselves, others, and their world. Many of the decisions are made subconsciously in the first few years of life when personality and character are forming. Research shows that the wallpaper of personality is formed in the first three to five years of life.

The child is constantly asking himself or herself, "Am I good or bad?" "Am I capable or not capable?" "Can I trust Mommy or not?" "Is the world safe or not?" Children are also making decisions about what they will do in the future, and this is also responsible for shaping personality. These decisions will determine if the child feels the need to survive or feels motivated to thrive in life.

Children often learn that mistakes are bad, and parents contribute to making children feel stupid, bad, inadequate, or like failures when they make mistakes. These negative contributions happen when parents use punishments or withdraw love when children behave poorly. Often this causes children to learn coping mechanisms such as lying or being secretive. Parents have the opportunity to change how children perceive mistakes by giving children the courage to be imperfect. Children should learn that all humans make mistakes and that we are all working for improvement rather than perfection.

I advise parents to help their children learn to humbly admit they are bound to make mistakes. This way, children learn to acknowledge their mistakes without a sense of loss in their personal value.

A child needs to sense that parents know how to separate the deed from the doer. A child's failures and bad behavior derive from a lack of skill. They do not change the child's personal value. It is healthier to help children see mistakes as opportunities to learn. If parents want to teach children to choose wisely, parents must give them opportunities to choose and, if necessary, make mistakes. Children can only learn through experiences.

A child who does not feel motivated to thrive will have his or her emotional, social, and intellectual development negatively impacted. Reinforcing a positive message in the early years about your child, the world, and others is crucial. Shame, blame, punishments, time-outs, and other parental actions help children feel badly about themselves, the world, and their parents. Young children see themselves through the eyes of the adults. The way parents speak to their children will become the way those children view themselves, and parents need to be sure to give children loving and compassionate inner voices.

Children Need Rhythm

Routine is to a child what walls are to a house: it gives boundaries and dimensions to his life…
It is the obligation of the parents to set up a routine within which the family can function
comfortably; to establish and maintain a daily order and let the children fall into line.
—Rudolf Dreikurs

Young children thrive when there is rhythm in their daily lives. Incorporating rhythm into the flow of the day so children know what to expect is important and shows respect for the child. Rudolf Steiner developed the Waldorf philosophy, and it strongly values rhythm. My daughter's Waldorf teacher taught me this essential concept. *Rhythm* has since become one of my most useful parenting tools.

Rhythm surrounds human beings—night and day, weekday and weekend, the yearly cycle of the seasons, and more everyday examples. We rely on internal rhythms such as breathing, the beating of our hearts, sleeping and waking, and digestion. Although we are such beings of rhythm, we have moved far away from following nature's rhythm or even being able to bring rhythm into our busy, modern lives. Electric lighting allows us to be awake as long as we like or need; washing machines allow us to do laundry whenever convenient; and telephone and e-mail allow us to get in touch with our friends at any time.

Rhythm in our lives gives us security and strength. However, we often only realize this in the absence of it. When our schedules become busy, unpredictable, and hectic, we feel stressed and can even become sick. If this can happen to adults (the makers of the schedules), imagine what the absence of rhythm can feel like for the young child who is shuffled from one activity and unfamiliar environment to the next and having to constantly adjust to something new. Young children are much more connected with rhythm, and they live and learn through repetition.

Unfortunately, many families report spending almost an hour putting their children to bed or spending early mornings nagging, reminding, and yelling to get their preschoolers out the door. What many parents don't realize is that a consistent rhythm can help with discipline challenges. Rhythm can regulate the child's sleeping and eating habits and can help parents and children with the transition from one activity to the next and can help avoid power struggles. Rhythm gives a child a sense of calm, security and structure.

In order to create rhythm, you might have to slow down, do less, have less, and keep your days simpler. This offers the child a peaceful sense of familiarity and the empowering sense of mastery over his or her schedule. As you create your family rhythm, try to create a flow of "breathing in" and "breathing out" activities throughout the day. The "in-breath" activities are short times of peace, quiet, and ritual such as coming together for breakfast, singing a grateful song before eating, having story time after coming in from playing outside, or having independent play-time after a busy afternoon of activities. These moments of peace and quiet throughout the day are soothing for all children. The "out-breath" activities are longer stretches of time in which the child can engage in play, exploration, and discovery such as having a play-date, a walk at the beach, or a trip to the playground or just free playtime. For example, we might go for a walk or hike as an "out-breath" activity in which the children can be free to explore and play. Following that, we might come together for a snack or for a story as an "in breath," and after that we have some free playtime as another "out-breath" activity.

To help your child remember the family rhythm, you can create a daily chart. I started by sitting down with my three-and-a-half-year-old and talking about our days. The next day I asked her to help me draw each item on the list we had come up with the day before. I did the drawing, and she colored them (you can simply take pictures of your child performing each daily activity). She helped me create a time line and tape it to the wall in our hallway. To help the child stay on task, you can simply say, "What is next on our rhythm chart?" or "This is what we do after dinner" Let the rhythm become the boss—not you.

The Need for a Prepared Environment

We can best help children learn, not by deciding what we think they should learn and thinking of ingenious ways to teach it to them, but by making the world, as far as we can, accessible to them, paying serious attention to what they do, answering their questions—if they have any—and helping them explore the things they are most interested in.
—John Holt

Parents and children are living in busy spaces and have busy lifestyles and schedules. Children can feel discouraged and humiliated when they want to help themselves, but adults make them feel too slow, unskilled, small, or inadequate to do things independently. Often, adults also go around fixing what their children have just attempted to do. Toddlers might be able to serve themselves, use breakables, and pour milk. However, it is more convenient and less messy for parents to do it for them.

Children develop through a natural process, and their curiosity guides them to learn and explore, which means children are active learners and motivated participants in their own education. Researchers have long emphasized that children's social, emotional, and cognitive skills are interrelated and develop within responsive, caring, and purposeful environments. A beautiful, safe, inviting, and thoughtfully arranged environment that conveys a sense of harmony and order can inspire, comfort, and empower children. This prepared environment can allow children to be involved in meaningful tasks from a very young age.

For the young child, even the simplest, most ordinary tasks can help the child practice valuable skills and can become the foundation for all academic subjects. For example, handwork, cooking, and table setting provide a hands-on, multisensory approach to math that teaches children to follow a series of steps using the concept and properties of numbers. Through dressing, preparing snacks, grasping, and pouring, children acquire the fine-motor skills that foster art and writing.

In order to meet the child's need for love and power, parents must help the child perceive himself or herself as a respected, appreciated family member and as capable of making a difference through meaningful contributions. I call this "having purpose." An optimum physical home environment for a young child promotes independence and autonomy and allows and empowers the child to perform activities and be in control of the environment. Such an environment lessens frustration and inspires the child to perform everyday tasks independently or with little help.

Young children benefit from functioning easily and accomplishing things on their own without feeling overwhelmed or overstimulated. Most importantly, a more purposeful home environment shows respect, consideration, and appreciation for the child, which helps build the child's confidence.

Part II—The Adult

Becoming a Purposeful Parent

I have come to the frightening conclusion that I am the decisive element. It is my personal approach that creates the climate. It is my daily mood that makes the weather. I possess tremendous power to make life miserable or joyous. I can be a tool of torture or an instrument of inspiration; I can humiliate or humor, hurt or heal. In all situations, it is my response that decides whether a crisis is escalated or de-escalated, and a person is humanized or de-humanized. If we treat people as they are, we make them worse. If we treat people as they ought to be, we help them become what they are capable of becoming.

—Haim G. Ginott

Every so often, a parent at my lectures says he or she was shamed, blamed, punished, rewarded, and more by his or her parents, and he or she still turned out fine. However, if we look at the high incidence of teen behavioral problems such as drug abuse, legal infractions, and even suicide, it becomes obvious that many of the old beliefs about parenting are not working. Has our society really turned out okay?

We are the most depressed, medicated, and addicted nation. Perhaps we might have turned out better if our parents had used a more purposeful approach to discipline. I am constantly asking parents to eliminate blame and shame, lecturing, rewards, praise, time-outs, threatening, bribing, nagging, and more from their parenting. They often look at me, discouraged. Some have even asked, "What is left for us to do?"

There are many alternative tools for parents looking for long-term, nonpunitive, nonpermissive, respectful, constructive, and loving parenting techniques. Parents can become more intentional. They can learn how to get to the core of their child's behavior, and they can bring more joy into parenting. Unfortunately, no single disciplinary method will be effective in every situation. What works today might not work tomorrow, and what works for one child might not work for the next. Take time to get to the core of your child's behavior to determine what method to use.

Many times I hear adults say that a child needs more discipline. What do they mean by *discipline*? Most adults mean the child needs more time-outs, punishments, lecturing, consequences, and taming. Sadly, *discipline* is often confused for *punishment*. However, discipline has nothing to do with punishment. It comes from the Latin word *disciplina* (to teach) and *discipulus* (disciple—a follower or student of a teacher, leader, or philosopher).

I jokingly say to my mother-in-law that I could "shape up" my children in just a few days. Praise, reward, punishment, shame, blame, lectures, and more do work in the short term, but do we want our children to do as we say and be "good" at the cost of their self-esteem, confidence, and self-worth? Should we attempt to get our children to behave well by building a disrespectful relationship with them or hurting them? Should we make them feel badly about themselves or us? Do we want them to please us in exchange for rewards and praise? Do we want them to fear us?

Disciplining a child has nothing to do with punishing a child. Punishing hurts and uses fear as a motivator. I often explain to parents that when children are punished, they feel two things—mad and guilty. When they feel guilty, they might develop feelings of inadequacy and low self-esteem. When children feel angry, they might develop feelings of revenge. We parents don't want our children to learn to feel badly about themselves or to feel badly about us, so why are so many parents using punishments?

When parents are planning for a baby's arrival, they are so full of love and want to do everything possible to set the child up for success. Parents change their diet, take birthing classes, start a college fund, and more. Fast-forward two years, and some of us are doing this:

- Yelling
- Blaming
- Shaming
- Praising
- Rewarding

- Threatening
- Bribing
- Nagging
- Lecturing
- Even spanking

What happened? Parents often punish because they want a sense of control. They don't want to be permissive, and they think the only option is punishment. They need to feel they are "doing something" instead of allowing their child to "get away with" misbehaving. Many parents still believe that, to avoid raising a spoiled or out-of-control child, they must be strict. They must overparent to prevent negative behavior.

Unfortunately parenting often gets polarized into strict or permissive. Either parents are strict and have "good" children, or parents are permissive and are raising brats. It does not have to be this way. There is a better, more positive and purposeful way to parent.

Inflicting punishment is a release for the adult's anger and frustration. However, parents realize punishment is disrespectful and does not work in the long term when they have to repeatedly punish their children for the same things or when they see the social-emotional damage it has caused.

Past experiences have conditioned some parents to believe children must suffer to learn, and those parents lack the knowledge and skills to use different methods. Our parenting beliefs usually stem from the way we were raised as children and what we have experienced from adults over the years. Many parents come from traditional backgrounds in which their parents used punishments for years. Now, for many parents, those tools just feel like second nature.

Often, parents come home from the hospital unprepared to raise a child. Learning what to do for the next eighteen years is a much-needed component to succeed in parenting. It is the parent's job to nurture a child's spirit, as adults set the emotional tone in the home.

I urge parents to better understand how children develop and learn in order to break outdated and unproductive beliefs about parenting and bad parenting habits that can negatively impact our children's social and emotional development. Parents can take advantage of brain research and new knowledge on child rearing to transform their parenting approach. We no longer need to parent based only on our intuition, cultural and evolutionary needs, and parenting tales passed down to us from our parents and grandparents.

Handle Conflict When You Are Calm

We can change our whole life and the attitude of people around us simply by changing ourselves.
—Rudolf Dreikurs

Have you noticed how your mental state can escalate a situation? I have reacted to a situation in which my child made a simple request, and I caused the situation to escalate to where both my child and I were having meltdowns. Checking in with yourself before you respond to your child is imperative to effective parenting. When we are stressed, we tend to be less emotionally available for our children and less tolerant of their challenging behaviors. Therefore, we cause situations to escalate more quickly.

As you tune into your emotional state, you must ask yourself some questions: What is my state of mind right now? Am I calm, loving, and accepting, or am I angry, frustrated, and critical? If you are not in a calm, loving, and accepting place, you will not accomplish much. Ask yourself, What do I need? Am I tired? Am I overwhelmed? Am I mad about something else? Taking care of ourselves first is crucial to being the compassionate parents we want to be. Taking time for ourselves is not selfishness. It is wisdom.

Dr. Daniel Siegel, the author of *Parenting from the Inside Out* and *The Whole-Brain Child*, uses a simple, concrete analogy to help us understand the brain. Imagine your brain is your hand. Hold it out in front of you with your palm facing toward you. Your wrist and the lower part of your palm represent your brain stem. This is where you regulate involuntary bodily functions such as your breathing, heart rate, and digestive system. Now bend your thumb so it folds over the palm of your hand. Your thumb represents your midbrain, which is responsible for your emotions, memories, and most flight, fight, or freeze responses. Next, bend your fingers over your thumb so you are making a fist.

The back of your hand and fingers (the whole fist) represent the outer surface of the brain, which is your brain cortex. The back area of the cortex is responsible for your senses. The section over your knuckles is the part of the brain where thinking takes place. The very front section by your fingernails is the area called the prefrontal cortex. It is close to both the midbrain and the brain stem. This front part of the brain regulates emotions, interpersonal relationships, response flexibility, intuition, mindsight, social cognition, self-awareness, morality, and more.

So what happens when you are stressed, overwhelmed, and sleep deprived, and your children are really pushing your buttons? You temporarily lose the ability to regulate your rational brain. Your prefrontal cortex is not functioning, and you lose the ability to regulate your emotions. You cannot sustain appropriate interpersonal relationships. Forget about intuition or being flexible. You might not even be aware of how inappropriate you are being in the moment.

The ability to get ourselves together again is a critical skill for both adults and children. But keep in mind that our children's brains will take about twenty-five years to completely develop. Therefore, young children may not yet have the ability to regulate their emotions or be flexible. With that said, who is responsible for our relationships with our young children? We are! We must take the time to calm down, regather, and access our rational brains before acting.

Remember those "mirror neurons" scientists have discovered? Children will imitate not only the way we act, but they will also imitate our emotional responses, and they will also sense our emotional state or that "negative vibe" we are sending off. Our children's "monkey see, monkey do" neurons will kick-in affecting the way they are, now, feeling. As we set the emotional climate, we can provide our children with the behavior we want them to learn and practice. We want to help our children learn those valuable social-emotional and life skills they will need for a successful life (remember that list of characteristics parents want their children to posses as young adults?) Emotional stability, self-regulation, anger management, kindness, respect are just a few of those important skills we can role-model daily. This brain in the palm of your hand representation is also a way for you to explain the concept to your young child (four years old or older).

Keep a Strong and Loving Attitude

We want to create an emotional climate that encourages children to cooperate because they care about themselves, and because they care about us. We want to demonstrate the kind of respectful communication that we hope our children will use with us—now, during their adolescent years, and ultimately, as our adult friends.
—Adele Faber and Elaine Mazlish

Many parents are not aware their actions can reinforce unproductive behavior. Even if they are aware, however, most don't know what to do to change to a more purposeful approach. For example, we have all seen the child in the grocery store who whines for sweets. Mom or Dad says no a few times, threatens to leave the store, and lectures on the cons of eating sugar. The child escalates the whining. The parents give in. The child gets the sweets along with the message that his or her behavior was successful. The parent has just reinforced the child's bad behavior.

Parents can attempt to stop bad behavior by threatening, yelling, or punishing, but the behavior either escalates or children learn to conform for fear of punishment. On the other hand, if we learn how to address the root causes of our children's poor behavior, we teach the children to develop important life skills.

For example, the child who wants the candy at the store and who is engaging you in a power struggle can learn several life skills if you try a few different approaches that are mutually respectful and that disengage you from the power struggle. One thing you can do is to connect with your child by saying, "We have such a sweet tooth. I can see why you would like a treat. Let's find a healthier treat," or "You seem hungry, let's pick out a fruit for you to snack on." This way, you don't have to fight or give in. Validate the child's feelings with, "I see you are upset with me because I said no." You can also give the child two acceptable choices of treats: "You can have the dried mango or the banana chips." Another effective strategy is to engage the child in something purposeful and invite the child to help: "We need three boxes of pasta. Can you get them for me?"

If the child is now having a tantrum, the mutually respectful thing to do might be to gently scoop him or her up and bring the child to the car (no need to lecture, shame, blame, threaten, or hurt). This is respectful to the child and to yourself. You send the child a message that you mean what you say, that you follow through, and that you are able to be kind and firm at the same time. When you use those tools, you model how to solve conflicts in a mutually respectful way. The child also learns resilience, patience, responsibility, self-regulation, and many more skills.

Effective discipline needs to be simultaneously rational and loving. It can't be controlling (I am the boss) or permissive (wishy-washy). It also can't go back and forth from controlling to permissive without consistency. Many parents feel they are too permissive until their children become out of control. Then the parents turn to yelling, threatening, or punishing until they hate being that type of parent, and they go back to being too permissive. This is a vicious cycle. This type of parenting is reactive. A purposeful parent is proactive by reflecting before acting instead.

A purposeful parent seeks long-term results, looks for solutions instead of blame, and realizes that the person who can and must change first is the adult. Children are resistant to authority and will rebel against it. It's much more effective to put your arm around your child when he or she is being resistant and say, "I see you are struggling. Let me help you." The goal is to teach life skills to the child while making sure the message of love gets through.

- When your child spills his or her juice, you can scream and wipe up the juice with anger, or you can help your child get a cloth and say, "Let's clean it up together."
- When your child is playing too roughly with the dog, the baby, a peer, or a sibling, you can scold, argue, nag, threaten, or yell. Or you can separate the two and tell them both, "You two can try again later when you are ready to play more gently." The parent will do this even if it seems silly to tell the dog or the baby. This is to avoid assigning the roles of bully and victim.
- When your toddler hits, you might hit back, yell, or threaten. Or you can take the toddler's hand and gently pat his or her hands and say, "Gentle hands. People like love."

By handling the bad behavior this way, you are not using punishment, being permissive, or ignoring the problem. You are actively involved in helping the child handle the situation better while staying calm, friendly, and respectful to the child and yourself.

Use Encouragement Instead of Praise and Rewards

We destroy the love of learning in children, which is so strong when they are small, by encouraging and compelling them to work for petty and contemptible rewards, gold stars, or papers marked 100 and tacked to the wall, or A's on report cards, or honor rolls, or dean's lists, or Phi Beta Kappa keys, in short, for the ignoble satisfaction of feeling that they are better than someone else.

—John Holt

Encouragement is effective and conveys that the child is already loved and good, as is. Encouragement helps a child develop self-love and the much-needed sense of unconditional love. When a child has positive experiences, he or she develops self-confidence and a sense of belonging and significance.

Unfortunately, praise and rewards are common parenting tools. As with many traditional parenting tools, praising and rewarding work well in the short term. Often a parent's goal is to manipulate the child's behavior and get him or her to "be good" and do what the parent wants. When children expect to be praised and rewarded, their confidence diminishes, and they start to crave affirmation or reaction from others. I often see toddlers already looking at their parents and expecting reactions or affirmations after performing an activity. Besides, praise and rewards can be dangerous in the long term. A young child wants to please the parents and seeks affirmation.

As the child grows, this changes. The child starts to look for affirmation from others outside the family and will eventually wish to please peers, teachers, significant others, and the "cool" kids. It is dangerous to raise a praise junkie because, to fit in or be approved, that child might cave in to peer pressure as peers become important people in his or her life. Children also often learn to manipulate parents for bigger and better rewards. Reward a child for doing something once, and you might never have the child doing it for free again.

It is easy to praise or reward children when they are behaving well, but how can we encourage children when they are behaving badly and not feeling good about themselves, which is when they need encouragement the most? Instead of praising, you can encourage by saying, "You did it," "You really tried hard," "I have faith you can handle this," or "I love you no matter what."

Children need feedback and appreciation for their hard work. However, do it substantially. Avoid empty compliments. For example, instead of, "Good job!" say, "I noticed you were focused while doing this puzzle." When the child shows you a drawing or coloring, instead of saying, "Beautiful picture," you can say, "I like the colors you used. Can you explain this work to me? What do you think we should call this artwork?"

This type of feedback also includes the social and emotional goals you might have for your child. When the child has a good playdate with someone, saying, "You were so good on the playdate," might be vague for the child. He or she could develop some confused or mistaken thoughts about what behavior was good. Instead, say, "Wow. I noticed how you were sharing with your friend today. Sharing with your friend today made the playdate fun for you and your friend." Substantial feedback will endorse emotional satisfaction and intellectual stimulation.

The goal is to help children learn to do what is right when no one else is watching—not simply because they have something to gain from it or because they seek to please people or crave recognition.

Let Them Hear the Love: Strategies to Close the Communication Gap

What do we say to a guest who forgets her umbrella? Do we run after her and say, "What is the matter with you? Every time you come to visit, you forget something. If it's not one thing, it's another. Why can't you be like your sister? When she comes to visit, she knows how to behave. You're forty-four years old! Will you never learn? I'm not a slave to pick up after you! I bet you'd forget your head if it weren't attached to your shoulders."
That's not what we say to a guest. We say, "Here's your umbrella, Alice," without adding "scatterbrain."
Parents need to learn to respond to their children as they do to guests.
—Haim G. Ginott

Don't we all enjoy winning an argument? Remember, though, when we want to win an argument, so do our children. It is a natural human desire. We must keep in mind that for us to win an argument, our children have to lose it. Many parents feel the need to hold the power and control the relationships with their children. That need, however, invites their children to constantly feel like losers. Often, parents use nonproductive tools when relating to their children such as wishing to be right, wanting to control the children, using revenge through punishments, withdrawing or stonewalling, venting endlessly, or being defensive.

I try to steer parents into what I consider more respectful and purposeful strategies, like these:

Refer to Yourself in the First Person

Use "I" to state your feelings, wishes, and hopes. Many times, parents talk to their children in the third person. They say things such as, "Mommy does not like it when you hit." It's as if Mommy is a separate entity. The child probably looks at you and thinks, "Who are you, then? Whom am I speaking to?" Simply say, "I don't like it when you hit me."

Agree to Disagree

You can say to your child that you might have to agree to disagree about a problem. State that you'll be happy to think about it and get back to the issue later. Don't allow your child to treat you disrespectfully. Say, "Stop. I can't work things out when I feel disrespected. Shall we try again later?" You can also ask, "What do you need from me to give me what I want?"

Articulate Feelings

Tell your child exactly how you feel. Teach your child that you cannot help unless you really know what is going on. When your child tells you a problem, you want to fix it. So a more helpful response would be something like this: "You feel _____ when _____, and you wish_____."

When your child says, "Annabelle is always taking my things," ask your child how he or she feels. Ask why.

Ask the child what he or she wishes would happen. Rephrase to ensure you understand: "You feel frustrated when Annabelle takes your things, and you wish she wouldn't."

Once the child articulates a feeling, that child is more ready to consider choices and feel empowered. That way, you are connecting with your child on an emotional level, and he or she feels supported and understood.

Approach the Child with Respect

We also need to make sure we are communicating with our children in a respectful way. It is so common for adults to communicate with children disrespectfully without even being aware of it. Adults disrespect children by using baby talk, talking down, talking about them as if they are not there, being condescending, faking excitement to stimulate interest, or using a phony sweet tone to win cooperation.

In the wintertime, I observed a caring dad telling his children in an annoyed tone of voice, "In or out? Get in quickly, or get out already!" He would then rush them in or out of the door to stop the house from cooling down.

I understand toddlers in their winter gear can be extra slow. I also understand this dad did not mean to be rude to the children. I simply asked him if he would talk that way to one of the guests as he or she lingered to come in or leave. Of course, he would not be unkind to a guest. He might kindly say, "Let me close the door and help you with your coat." Often we save our patience and kindness for others and lack it when speaking with the ones who matter the most to us.

Find out if you are being respectful to your child by asking yourself if you would speak that way to a coworker or colleague. Very often parents say, "You are fine," when their child falls down and gets hurt. Would we say the same to a coworker who just tripped and fell? Most people would say, "Are you okay? Let me help you." We must talk to our children as we talk to others, remembering that respect is not a privilege.

Say More with Less

Often, it is best to say less. My daughters' Waldorf teacher taught me to use an economy of words when requesting something of young children. Now when I say "helpers," they know it means I started a project, and I would like them to join me and find ways to contribute. "Clean and shine" means it is time to end the play and begin tidying up the house before dinner. Purposeful parenting is about saving our words to talk about how wonderful our children are or to engage in productive, interesting conversations with them instead of spending too much time nagging, reminding, explaining, and bargaining.

Not Everything Is Up for Discussion

If there is something your child *must* do, don't ask if he or she *wants* to do it. Just kindly say, "It is time to get into your car seat," "It is lunchtime," or "We clean up our toys before we eat dinner." Another common mistake is to yell instructions from across the room. It is more efficient to walk toward the child and get down to his or her eye level while you are talking.

Use Positive Directives

When your child is doing something you don't want, tell him or her what to do instead of what *not* to do. Say "gentle hands" instead of "don't hit" or "walk slowly" instead of "don't run." When children hear the negative statement, the very thing we do not want them to do is reinforced. When we say "don't run," the last thing he or she hears is "run," and that is what sticks in his or her mind. Positive message such as "stop," "slow down," or "loving hands" are much clearer and easier for the child to follow.

Ask Genuine Questions

Another common practice is for parents to trap children by asking a question they already know the answer to. Asking "Did you wash your hands?" "Did you flush?" "Did you clean up your room?" "Did you brush your teeth?" when you already know the child did not do it is disrespectful. Say, "I notice you did not brush your teeth," "I notice you did not clean your room," "I notice you forgot to wash your hands."

Accept the Child's Feelings

If your child is jealous of the new baby, take his or her feelings seriously. Instead of trying to talk the child out of those feeling by saying, "You don't have to feel jealous. You know I love you," you can say, "I see this is hard for you, and I love you." It is important parents get into a child's world and try to understand and respect his or her point of view. This shows that the parents genuinely care and are curious about their child instead of trying to mold him or her to fit those parents' values, hopes, and dreams.

Apologize and Move Forward

Explain to your child that everybody makes mistakes, but it takes courage to say, "I am wrong, and I am sorry." It is important to learn to recover from mistakes with a feeling of responsibility instead of blame, shame, and fear. Practicing apologizing and resolving problems together is key. Model this by apologizing to your child when you make a mistake or for past mistakes. This will prevent hurt feelings or seeds of mistrust between you and your child.

Choose a Method and Follow Through

Parents are responsible for the relationships with their children, and the adults can learn to change themselves instead of trying to control or change their children. It is more successful if you decide what you will do instead of what you will make your child do. You can improve a situation by having the courage to follow through and allow your child to learn from his or her behavior. Instead of saying, "Stop hurting the baby and go to your room," gently take the child by the hand and say, "Being always kind can be tricky, and I will not let you hurt people."

Here is what following-through looks like. First you must give the matter your full attention. Next, validate your child's feelings. Then, say how you feel and set your boundaries. Then, decide what you will do and follow through with action.

Here's an example: Tell your child you can see he or she is having a hard time waiting for you to finish a phone call. Say you get frustrated and distracted when he or she whines and screams at you as you are talking on the phone. Say you will walk away and finish your conversation somewhere more peaceful next time. When the occasion comes, simply walk away. Don't say a word or appear to be angry. Just lock yourself in your room, bathroom or outside, and finish the phone call. Come back and say nothing.

This technique only works when we skip the nagging, reminding, and lecturing. Make sure your words and actions match. If you say you will no longer pick up the toys, but then you hunt through the living room for items to be put away because you are worried about what guests will think, your words and actions are not matching. Children learn quickly to ignore words when they don't match actions.

Another key tool is to simply follow through with action instead of talk. It is perfectly fine for you to gently take your child by the hand and start walking, pick him or her up and carry him or her to bed, or take him or her back to the car when he or she is having a fit in the supermarket. The disrespectful option is to yell, nag, lecture, beg, order, or threaten. We must learn to think before demanding compliance, and then we need to follow through with kind and firm actions.

Make Time for Special Time

Earlier I mentioned humans are goal oriented and we are always seeking belonging and significance. Have you ever spent one hour doing something that should take twenty minutes because you had to stop to handle sibling fights, a whining toddler grabbing your legs, or other attention-seeking behaviors? You can stand there trying to cook dinner for an hour while a toddler clings and whines, or you can sit with him or her for five minutes, meet the need for love and belonging, and then finish dinner more quickly while he or she plays independently again.

Therefore, a powerful and proactive tool for lessing attention-seeking behaviors is creating "special one-on-one time" with your child. Your child regularly needs time alone with you. Even ten minutes twice a day of undivided attention can refuel the child's love "baskets." There is a direct relationship between time invested in special one-on-one time (in which you are available physically, emotionally, and spiritually) and your child's behavior. In the absence of positive, undivided attention, children will demand attention with negative attention-seeking behaviors (tantrums, whining, picking fights with siblings, interrupting, and more).

As you consistently implement special one-on-one time, you will see the attention-seeking behaviors begin to diminish. That means less time hassling over frustrating misbehaviors. Consistency is key here. The child must be able to count on it, so schedule standing dates in your calendar for this very special time with each of your children. One of the best things I did was to get my husband and the girls gift cards to a rock-climbing gym. For years he has been taking one of the girls climbing on the weekends, and I know he and the girls enjoy and look forward to this special time together. We must also remember that this is time spent doing something of the child's choice, and we need to be available in mind, body, and soul. Avoid running errands as a special time with your child and remember to turn off your phone.

Besides having a special date on the weekend, it is helpful to plan your daily rhythm making room for a couple of brief one-on-one time with each child throughout the day. I often try to make good use of ordinary moments to transform them into extraordinary ones. Getting in the tub with your toddler, giving a ten-minute back massage, sitting down to color a picture, or building with blocks are all ways you can give your child the quality time he or she craves. All children wants is to spend time with us. Don't forget to make this special time fun for both you and your child. What people enjoy doing together, brings them together.

Build Good Memories

Based on my studies of transactional analysis by Eric Berne, I have learned that every healthy person operates in three alter ego states. These states are called parent, adult, and child.

The parent state of personality is the ingrained voice of authority. It comes from years of conditioning by parents, teachers, coaches, neighbors, elders, or others in positions of authority. We might find ourselves in this state with children, spouses, students, or even people we manage at work. When we communicate with others in the "parent ego state," we're usually ordering, directing, and correcting with phrases such as, "Don't forget to put on your coat," "Finish your dinner," or "Clean up your toys."

The adult state of personality is a nonemotional, rationally thinking state. We operate in this ego state when we're thinking, reasoning, and processing information. This is the state you are in right now as you sit and read this book or when you are at work, in meetings, and in other nonemotional adult-to-adult interactions. Children operate in the "adult ego state" when they are absorbed in activities or in their play.

The child state of personality represents a highly emotional state. On the positive side of the child ego state, you might laugh hard or jump up and down after that promotion or a special awaited phone call. On the negative side, you might have a breakdown, throw a tantrum, display road rage, and more. Adults spend little time in the "child ego state." However, children spend most of their time in this highly emotional state.

Most parents agree that the majority of their communication with their children happens in the parent ego state—ordering, correcting, and directing. If you spend most of your time in the parent ego state, you might find yourself frequently engaged in power struggles with your child. Nobody (adult or child) wants to be told what to do, when to do it, or how to do it. Too much ordering, correcting, directing, or reminding often results in power struggles, because the natural reaction is to fight back. Children dislike being bossed around, and they tell parents so with tantrums, back talk, arguing, negotiating, and other bad behaviors.

Having fun with our children more often can be an effective parenting tool for preventing poor behavior. Interact less from the parent ego state (ordering, correcting, and directing) and interact more from the adult ego state (exploring, talking, engaging in activities together) and from the child ego state (playing, rolling around, and laughing together). Interacting and communicating in this way reduces power struggles, increases cooperation, and improves relationships. Most importantly, this kind of interactions is what creates strong emotional connections and positive memories.

Part III—The Environment

Learning through Everyday Life

Never help a child with a task at which he feels he can succeed.
—Dr. Maria Montessori

Sierra is busy throughout the whole morning. She carefully clips flowers, neatly arranges them in vases, and places the vases beautifully around the classroom. She then takes a banana from the fruit basket, slices it, and serves it to the class. After washing the dishes and cleaning up her banana-slicing work, she cheerfully sits next to a friend and polishes a penny by rubbing vinegar and salt on it with a Q-tip. Sierra is three years old.

Sierra attends a Montessori preschool where she takes care of the environment, wipes up her spills, arranges flowers, and makes her own snacks. Purposeful learning is a hallmark of Montessori education. It recognizes that children's cognitive growth and development require respect for individuality and fulfillment of the needs of the "whole child." Dr. Maria Montessori's pioneering work created a blueprint for nurturing all children (from gifted to learning disabled) to become self-motivated, independent, lifelong learners.

Parents come to me for help with bedtime and mealtime battles or battles over clothing and destructive behaviors. Many parents are concerned about their child's lack of attention, confidence, organization, or independence. Through working with families, I have discovered that inadequate home environments cause many parenting issues. Many homes are too busy, cluttered, and overstimulating. If you want your child to be calm, to concentrate, and to develop attention, you must create an environment that is beautiful, clean, and full of soft colors, soothing music, and simple decoration. It should be a home cleared of clutter and with fewer choices—an environment like a spa.

A child needs chances to perform simple everyday tasks on his or her own to feel meaningful. It is crucial that the child is involved in the daily family activities. Washing fruits and vegetables; setting or clearing a table; watering plants; sorting, folding, and putting away laundry; sweeping; or helping in the garden help the child become a contributing member of the family.

When children are offered specially prepared environments that meet their needs, they feel taken under consideration, important, and appreciated as family members. They feel as if they are loved and truly belong. The physical environment can help young children feel encouraged and empowered. They feel they have autonomy and personal power. When children experience those positive feelings, they are reassured that they possess that love and power everyone craves. Parents can quickly witness power struggles diminish as a child's independence, self-help skills, and confidence increase.

Welcome to My Purposeful Home

As I walk you through my home, you will see that transforming the home environment to accommodate and include your child is easier than you might think. You will also notice that it is different from child-proofing a home. I once went to a family's home for an initial consultation to help them with their home environment, and I could see they were confused. The dad said right away, "We already have the house ready for our children. In fact, this house is all about the kids now," as he pointed around to the gates around the fireplace, by the stairs, and around the entertainment set. He also pointed out all the toys and gadgets in the living room and in the kitchen eating area.

Childproofing a home is important if you have young children, but what I propose goes further and deeper. Child-preparing the home is creating not only a safe home, but a safely accessible home. One of the goals is to create a "yes" environment instead of a space where you have to say "no" constantly and you have to chase, monitor, interfere, and interrupt the child's exploration because of the many dangers. It is also important to avoid an environment in which the child has to depend on the help of the adult for most tasks because of inaccessibility.

One mom of a toddler and a preschooler told me, "My children simply come in and drop their jackets and backpack by the front door and expect me to take care of it." First, I asked if there is a designated space for those items, and she said yes. Then I asked how accessible this space is for the children. She answered, "Not really, since it is the hangers in the front hallway closet or the high hooks in the mudroom." Well, that explains something. If she had said it was accessible, then my next question would be, "Have you taken time to show, model, and practice the skills with your children?"

For example, right by the entrance, a small chair can be placed for the child to sit while putting on and taking off his or her shoes. A child thrives when things are accessible. A child can have a place to hang his or her coat and a place to store shoes, hats, and gloves. A child needs the opportunity to practice these meaningful and simple everyday tasks. A child can develop hand-eye coordination, concentration, and fine-motor coordination by simply practicing buttoning, zipping, lacing, and other dressing skills.

Basically, all things need to have a place, and this place needs to be easily accessible to the child, and the adult needs to take time for practicing. With those three things in place, parents can witness chaos, dependency, and power struggles diminish as a child's independence, self-help skills, and confidence increase.

The kitchen is the best area in the home for a young child to feel purposeful and to perform meaningful work. A child must be given the tools and freedom to help out in the kitchen and be encouraged to prepare his or her own snacks. Place the child's food on the bottom drawer or shelf in the refrigerator so he or she can help out with food preparation and table setting. With little help and a bit of mess, children are able to slice a banana, make orange juice, or put together a sandwich. Even toddlers can scoop dry cereal into a bowl, pour milk from a small jar, and serve blueberries with small tongs.

A low cabinet allows child to help set the table

Many moms I work with explain that they have to resort to television or other media to keep their children busy and safe while they get dinner ready. Purposeful kitchen environments, however, provide many ways to engage children. Children and parents can get dinner ready together while strengthening the relationship. This way, in the future when grown children come home for Thanksgiving, they will hopefully enjoy their parents' company and help set the table instead of watching TV or staring at their phones until dinner is served.

A Low Cabinet

A low cabinet can hold your child's cups, utensils, and snacks. Allow the child to prepare his or her snacks and help with meal preparation duties such as pouring, measuring, and stirring. Progressive approaches to education encourage children, whenever possible and safe, to handle beautiful and breakable materials. This shows respect and trust as you share with your child what the rest of the family uses—pottery, glass, metal, and real utensils. Research shows there is a great increase in the self-respect of a child when he or she is allowed to use "real" things instead of plastic substitutes.

There is also a corresponding respect and care for the items when they are beautiful and breakable. In my house, my children always used glass, and we only had two breaks. Parents must take time for training. That means showing a child how to carry objects with both hands, walk slowly, and take one item at a time. Remind your child that accidents happen, and when glass breaks, he or she should step away and let a grown-up do the cleanup.

Snack on lower shelf of refrigerator.

Cleaning Tools

Giving the child his or her own cleaning supplies is empowering and also sets the tone for future collaboration with chores. He or she can use a cleaning cloth and a small spray bottle with a homemade all-purpose cleaner of water, vinegar, and tea tree essential oil. Children love spraying and wiping cabinet doors, the table, and the refrigerator. There are many child-sized brooms, dusters, and other cleaning tools that can also be incorporated as your child grows.

Aprons, Bibs, and Smocks

Child-sized aprons, bibs, and smocks on low pegs are also important. I don't use these only to keep my children clean. Putting on and removing an apron marks the beginning and end of an activity cycle and makes the child's work special. It also works as a visual cue and reminds the child to stay on task

Child-sized cleaning supplies.

Using a safe stepping stool.

Safe Stepping Stool

A safe stepping stool empowers the child and promotes independence. This stool allows the child to reach the countertop and sink for washing dishes, fruits, and veggies. It supports him or her when cooking. Allowing children to help with everyday activities such as making snacks, cleanup, and food preparation will help them learn to follow directions, measure, and count. It will also develop their fine and gross motor skills to improve hand-eye coordination and concentration. Food preparation also helps children learn self-help skills and empowers them to be independent and purposeful.

Small Table and Chair

Children must eat at tables and in chairs that allow them to sit up straight with their feet flat on the floor. This arrangement will promote good posture, but it will also help to develop balance, coordination, and concentration. When children feel grounded and balanced, they will be better able to control their bodies and stay on task for longer periods of time.

Many parents complain about how restless their children are and how hard it is to get them to sit still. Often their children are sitting on chairs that are either too tall or short. The children's feet are dangling in the air, or their knees are crunched. The small table and chair are useful for independent snack time and for food preparation activities.

It is important for a child to sit at the table with the family at least once a day to build the family relationship, practice table manners, watch your good role modeling, and build joyful memories.

Helping out at mealtimes

Snack Preparation

A young child might have a hard time opening a heavy jar of peanut butter, spreading jelly with a large butter knife, or handling a large bag of sliced bread. However, when the snack is set up in a more simple way, the child feels encouraged and empowered. A tray will help him or her carry everything to the small table and will keep the mess contained. The peanut butter and jelly can be portioned into small containers, and a child-sized food spreader is perfect for small hands. Similar arrangements can be made for banana slicing, juicing oranges, chopping vegetables, and other food preparation tasks. You can find resources and a list of child-sized kitchen utensils, dishes, glasses, and more on my website (www.thepurposefulchild.com).

Snack preparation

Mealtime should nourish both the body and soul. It should also help the family foster relationships. Unfortunately, mealtimes often become a time for correcting, nagging, threatening, and fighting.

Lighting a candle and singing a blessing are good ways to start a meal. The candle adds a visual cue to help the child stay on task. Young children love blowing the candles out at the end of the meal, and this also promotes and reinforces the important and soothing family rhythm and rituals.

Children will eat better if parents don't insist on their eating everything on their plates or tasting every food. Not forcing children to eat and not rewarding children with food, sweets, or dessert will foster a healthier relationship with food. When parents give children a lot of undue attention for refusing to eat something, they invite power struggles. There are only a few areas in which a young child has absolute power, and eating is one of them.

The best parents can do is provide only healthy choices and allow children to serve themselves and choose from those healthy foods. Make mealtime a priority in the daily routine. (Eating at the table at set times benefits children.) Be a good role model of healthy eating habits and proper table manners. Mealtime is also a time to share the good feelings of being together as a family.

A Place to Rest

A small selection of toys and books can be kept in the bedroom. Displaying them within easy reach of the child on attractive trays or baskets will give the child something to do upon waking and before falling asleep. On the other hand, too many options and over-stimulating toys and books in the bedroom can be distracting and overwhelming. Keep in mind you want to create a peaceful, simple bedroom where the main purpose is restful sleep. Use soft colors, minimize clutter, and keep it simple and calming.

Many parents come to me for help with bedtime battles. When I ask to see the child's room or for the parents to describe it to me, I can easily see why they have problems. Children's bedrooms are overstimulating and overwhelming. There are bright colors on walls, curtains, and bedding. Too many bright toys, books, stuffed animals, and more fill the spaces. Some rooms even have sound machines, night-lights, and other battery-operated items as well as posters, pictures, and decorations hanging on walls. No wonder the child does not want to go to sleep. Who would?

"I can help you put laundry away, mom"

Low Bed

A child thrives in an environment that promotes peaceful, independent rest. The child's bed should be a place where he or she can independently climb into and out of when he or she is ready to crawl. If you provide a very low bed or mattress on the floor in a safe room, your child will have a clear view of the surroundings and the freedom to explore. A low bed helps develop coordination, independence, and self-regulation.

The child is able to crawl out of bed, reach for a toy or book, and entertain himself or herself as well as crawl back into bed and put himself or herself to sleep after a period of play. This arrangement prevents the common problem of crying from boredom or exhaustion, and it eliminates the dangers of having a crib. Be mindful that the entire room must be childproof, and a gate should be placed at the door. This way, the room will work as a safe and large playpen.

"I can put myself to sleep."

Unbrakable Mirror

A nonbreakable mirror near the bed or play mat allows the baby to watch his or her reflection to learn more about his or her body. This also encourage movement (such as stretching muscles, pushing up, and reaching) and foster spacial awereness.

Hanging the mirror at the child's eye level is also helpful as the child gets older to foster self-help skills such as face wiping, nose blowing, and hair brushing. Many families have added low mirrors in the dining rooms where their children can check their faces and independently clean themselves up after meals.

Closet and Dresser

When setting up your child's closet, be sure clothing is hung at the child's eye level. A child-sized dresser or a stool to facilitate the opening and closing of drawers will encourage your child to get dressed and even put his or her laundry away while promoting autonomy and independence. A simple bedside table used as a dresser and a pressure rod in the closet at eye level (move it up as he or she grows) can empower the child and eliminate power struggles over clothing.

Mirrors and pictures at the child's eye level.

Besides removing clutter throughout the house, it is powerful to simplify the child's wardrobe. Having only a few items of each type of clothing makes the space less cluttered and makes the child more capable of independently making choices about what to wear. For example, our children only have about six shirts, six pairs of pants, six pairs of socks, two sweaters to go with everything, four pairs of pajamas, one coat, and two pairs of shoes. They also have their rain and winter gear.

Accessible closet with fewer choices.

Having only the things out that you would be okay with your child wearing eliminates arguments over dressing. If you don't want him or her to wear summer clothes in the winter, make sure you put those summer clothes away. If you don't want him or her wearing winter boots in the summer, put them away. Having out only a manageable amount of clothing in the closet allows the child to make appropriate choices and keep things organized more independently.

Self-Care Made Simple

Even the bathroom can provide opportunities to develop independence, self-help, and organizational skills. A step stool under the sink helps the child wash his or her hands and brush his or her teeth and hair with little to no help. A low mirror and a hand-wash station at the child's level can also be implemented. The bathroom is a great place for a laundry basket. When your child gets undressed, he or she will have a designated place to put dirty clothes. A small chair or step stool helps a child get undressed, since it is easier to remove and put on socks and pants when sitting down. The potty should have a place in the house from the beginning so your child gets used to seeing it and becomes naturally curious. This helps the child assimilate potty learning habits earlier.

"I can take care of myself"

Positive Potty Learning Tools

Young children only have a few areas where they can exercise absolute power and control. Some of these areas include eating, sleeping, and potty training. Children don't want to be trained. They want to learn. Approach potty training as potty learning, and do it gently and respectfully.

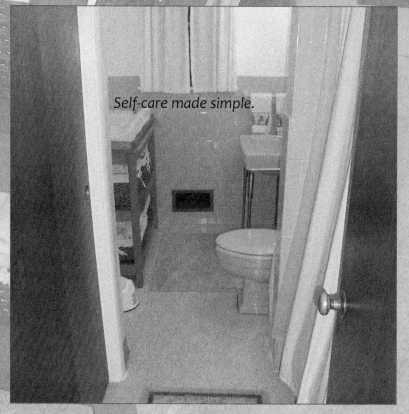

Self-care made simple.

If your toddler did not use cloth diapers, and the potty is new in your home, start to build pre-toilet learning skills by putting a cloth pad or cotton underwear inside his or her disposable diaper to give more feedback when wet. Every time the child feels the wet sensation, he or she will be building an understanding of toilet behavior. When children are able to stand or walk, diapers can be changed standing up and always in the bathroom. He or she can start to practice taking his or her pants down while sitting on the potty and putting pants back up without pressure.

Every time your child has a soiled diaper, you can place the poop in the toilet and say, "Poop goes in the potty." Encourage your child to flush it. This way the transition for your child from being changed to changing himself or herself will be much smoother.

Avoid praising and rewarding when your child succeeds at going in the potty. When your child expects to be praised or rewarded, his or her confidence diminishes. Give your child feedback, and show appreciation for his or her hard work, by saying, "Wow! You just used the potty," or "You got your pants down all by yourself today."

If your child has an accident, do not blame, shame, punish, or show frustration. Just say in a matter-of-fact tone, "Pee goes in the potty," and then gently encourage your child to be part of the cleanup by having him or her fetch new clothes. The goal is to help the child potty learn independently in a respectful, empowering way. This will develop the child's confidence and independence and will promote emotional satisfaction.

"I am learning to use the potty."

As I was in bed nursing my newborn, my three-year-old shouts from the hallway, "Mom, Annabelle [two years old] pooped on the floor." I took a breath and shouted back, "I will be right there, give me two minutes." I walked out of the room a few minutes later, looking for the poop, and could not find it.

I asked, "Girls, what happened to the poop?"

Pollyanna replied, "I cleaned it up, Mom."

"Really? How did you do it?"

"I just picked it up with the paper and flushed it away like you do it," she said.

Shocked, I responded, "Great! Where was it so I can spray the floor?"

She walked over and pointed, "It was around here, but I already wiped it [with her own cleaning supplies and child-sized tools]."

I was amazed. All the time I have been spending preparing the environment and practicing everyday tasks with them was starting to pay off.

Realizing the peculiarly absorbent nature of the child's mind, she has prepared for him a special environment; and, then, placing the child within it, has given him the freedom to live in it, absorbing what he finds there….The first aim of the prepared environment is, as far as it is possible, to render the growing child independent of the adult. That is, it is a place where he can do things for himself—live his own life—without the immediate help of adults.
—Dr. Maria Montessori

Playing with a Purpose

Our highest endeavor must be to develop free human beings who are able of themselves to impart purpose and direction to their lives. The need for imagination, a sense of truth, and a feeling of responsibility—these three forces are the very nerve of education.

—Rudolf Steiner

Young children seek sensory input, movement, order, and the freedom to choose activities and explore them deeply without interruption. Carefully prepared, calm, simple, and beautiful environments help children choose well. Children learn to choose activities, stay on task, and clean up when their toys and activities are displayed in a more intentional way. Placing them on open shelves in attractive trays or baskets within easy reach allows the child to see what is available.

Hands-on, simple, and open-ended toys.

When finished with a task or toy, he or she can easily put any work back on the shelf where it will be accessible the next time. Remaining toys can be put away into a toy closet for rotation, and older children can be involved in the rotation of materials and setup of the play space.

Purposeful Toys

Bodily exploration and constructive and creative play are considered the most important "work" of the young child and the activities through which the child grows physically, intellectually, and emotionally. With good house toys, the child learns how to think, concentrate, solve problems, and control the use of his or her body and hands. Simple, open-ended, multipurpose, and natural materials make for the best toys.

Wooden blocks, silks, and wooden animals.

Children learn from concrete to abstract, known to unknown, and simple to complex concepts. For example, if you have a new book with pictures of fruits and vegetables, take your child to the kitchen to handle, smell, and taste a piece of fruit. Then go look at the pictures of fruits in the book. This way, intelligence is built upon a wealth of experience.

Intentionally surround your child with natural materials, handmade and unformed, so the child's imagination is actively involved in play. Transforming the object into what is needed for play asks the child to be a creative thinker and to be fully engaged with head, hands, and heart. For example, a simple cloth doll with not much detail to the face can help children to project and process their own feelings while playing. They can imagine the doll is sad or happy or mad or afraid. If the doll is a plastic realistic replica of a little girl with a pleasing smile and expression, it is harder for the child to imagine and pretend the doll is crying or sad or surprised.

Children process their own lives and realities in their pretend play, so the simpler unformed figures give the child more possibilities for creativity and imagination.

It is better for the child to be actively engaged with a toy than passively pushing buttons on plastic and battery-operated ones. When picking a new toy, keep in mind that active toys encourage children to be passive, and passive toys

Handmade fairy dolls

encourage children to be actively engaged in learning.

I have witnessed how children can play for hours (and over years) with wooden blocks, cloth dolls, wagons, pushcarts, rocks, pieces of fabrics, and other simple items. My children have few toys and only a few toys out at a time. Most of the toys we have out do not even need to be rotated often. My children can play with them every day in a different way. The wooden blocks have been out for years. One day they are used as a farm. The next they are a zoo, house, or playground. Sometimes small toy animals or small wooden peg people are incorporated. A couple scarves of mine have become part of dressing up, slings and wraps for baby wearing, hammocks for their animals or babies, and much more. A basket of play silks or cloths, clothespins, and a piece of rope turn into a tent in a few minutes and into an entire afternoon of fun.

Play-silks as dress-up.

Story Time

Early language and literacy begin in the first years of life. Storytelling fosters creativity and imagination. Simple puppets and prompts can enrich this experience. When setting up a reading corner, reading materials should face the child. Books look more interesting and inviting that way. Often books are arranged "library style" and at times even up on a high shelf. But consider this: a young child is not able to read the side of any book yet. Many children can spot their favorite books from across the room, so children can be set up for success by having books on shelves where they can access them easily and independently.

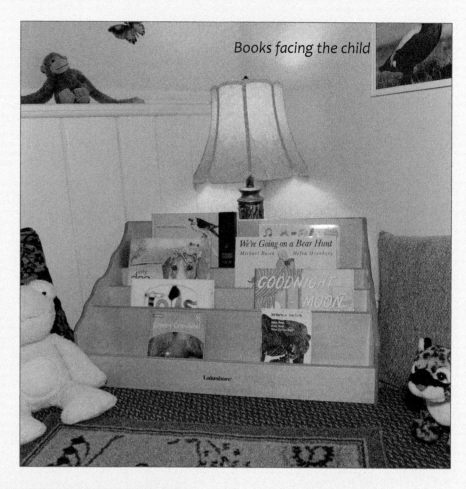

Books facing the child

Wall Art and Pictures

Children feel appreciated, respected, and encouraged to explore and learn when wall art, pictures, and mirrors hang at eye level. This principle can be applyed not only in the child's bedroom, but throughout the home.

Small Table and Chair

As I mentioned before, children must "work" at a table and chair that allow them to sit up straight with their feet flat on the floor. Drawing, coloring, and crafts are best done sitting at a table. (Easels and blackboards are useful too.) This will help foster good posture and balance as well as skills such as coordination and concentration needed for academic work.

Eye-level pictures.

The "Work" Mat

This concept I bring from my classroom experience as a Montessori teacher. The use of a work mat is useful when playing and working for the following reasons:

- It marks the work space just as a table would, which brings the child's focus to the activity and keeps him or her on task longer.
- It helps the child stay organized and keeps materials and toys from being scattered all over the floor. Gently remind your child that his or her work should stay on the mat.
- It also teaches the child to respect the work of a sibling. You can say, "This is not your work mat. Please ask your brother if you may touch his puzzle."
- If your child is in the middle of a longer activity or project that has to be interrupted, the work on the mat can be neatly saved for later use.

"A work mat helps me stay organized and focused."

This tool also helps handle problems with sharing or sibling rivalry. In addition to having a work mat for each child, you can use a picture or a name card for each. The children will soon learn to respect the objects of others when those objects are on a mat or when they have name cards on them. Use place mats for small toys and activities and a small area rug for larger activities. Many of my clients have had success with this tool.

The Work Cycle

Children often have a strong sense of order, and they thrive when there is a rhythm to be followed. Encourage children to choose an activity off the shelf, play, clean up, and put it away before moving on to the next activity.

Following this model is not initially easy with young children. However, as adults model the behavior and stay consistent, children pick up the pattern over time, and the work cycle becomes a natural routine. I also often recommend parents take pictures of the toys and activities and attach these to the bottom of the shelf or onto the baskets. That way, children have visual cues of where things go, and this helps eliminate constant nagging and reminding from the adult.

Purposeful Time-Out

A more purposeful type of time-out can be an encouraging and empowering experience for you and your child. It even teaches valuable life skills. Most Montessori classrooms have a peace area. This space is usually a corner, table, or small rug where children's feelings are validated, and they can feel better. Children should be involved in making this space by decorating it and bringing items they enjoy such as peaceful books or toys.

"Sometimes I want to be alone in a quite space."

Often parents believe they must address bad behavior right away or the child won't know why he or she is being reprimanded. Parents do not want the child to get away with misbehaving. However, we now know that allowing time to calm down and waiting to address an issue when everyone (including you) can be respectful and receptive is more effective. If you want to teach a lesson, take some time to calm down first. Children will experience increased self-esteem as they learn to problem solve, control their emotions, and foster their relationships with those around them.

Sadly, a punitive and isolating type of time-out is the most-used method of discipline by parents today. Many parents believe guilt, shame, and suffering will motivate children to behave better. Children, however, do better when they feel better. I often tell my clients that time-outs invite three things from their children—negative feelings about themselves (believing they are bad instead of understanding what they are doing is bad), sneaky behavior as they find ways to be more careful about not getting caught, and negative feelings about the adult as they seek revenge and plot how to get even.

When the child is experiencing behavior challenges, ask if it would be helpful to go to that cool of space you both created. If your child is too upset and says no, ask if the child would like you to go with him or her. If your child still says no, you can say, "Okay. I will go." Then go somewhere that brings you peace. This is a great model for the child.

Empower your child to self-manage inappropriate behavior and solve conflicts by sitting with your child and communicating your feelings, needs, and frustration. The peace area is a place for reflection, conflict resolution, cooling off, and feeling better. It is not a punitive time-out or isolation of the child. Children can use it to solve conflicts, enjoy a peaceful moment, or practice control of their bodies and emotions.

Creating a peace area in your home will help your child acquire and foster conflict resolution skills as well as develop language and self-control. Creating a peace area (or a break space) can help a child learn to self-regulate when solving problems during times of intense frustration or anger. Using the peace area for a break allows the child some distance from the angering event and the time to access his or her rational brain. This helps the child be more able to compromise and problem solve with you, siblings, or peers. The peace area also lessens, if not eliminates, the social and emotional cost a disrespectful conflict can cause.

Parents often talk, do, and problem solve too much for the child. Parents must practice quiet observation in order to learn the child's interests, strengths, and weaknesses. Children need repetition and profound concentration. These are, after all, the moments of self-construction in which children are forming knowledge and personalities.

A child needs to be loved and hugged, and a child needs to laugh when playing games with adults. But a child also needs freedom from the adult—freedom to self- construct. When engaged in an activity, the child should be protected from interruptions from siblings or other family members. When he or she seems absorbed in an activity, stand at a distance. Let him or her finish the activity before walking in and interrupting. A child does not need interference, direction, or correction unless he or she is misusing an activity or toy or is in danger of getting hurt or hurting others.

Getting married. We came home with candied almonds wrapped in tule and a centerpiece from a wedding. Worth hours of fun.

A child must be able to explore and make mistakes. Children learn more through trial and error than if adults show the solution or provide the right answer. Parents are often amazed to see how focused a child can become when concentration is not interrupted.

A child has a reason for every displayed behavior (even if that behavior seems odd). Be curious about what your child is doing. Take guesses about how he or she might be learning from this experience. Ask why he or she is doing something. It is amazing to hear a child's justification. Having a conversation about play creates an environment in which the child feels supported and safe to explore and be creative.

I once walked in on my two-and-a-half-year-old throwing her pretend fruits and vegetables all over the living room. She was repeatedly throwing handfuls of them. The first thing that crossed my mind was, "This is not right." However, I stopped myself, watched, and waited. I had to fight the urge to stop her or reprimand her for "mistreating" her toys.

When she was done, I calmly asked her what she was doing. She looked at me with a smile and said, "Mommy, I just fed all the animals. I am the zookeeper." She had a rational reason for throwing the play food, and if I had stopped her, I would have interrupted her concentration and crushed her spirit and creativity for no good reason.

You might be thinking, *How am I ever going to get out of the house if I am not supposed to interrupt my child?* I know there are times when parents have to interrupt their children's free play. They have to get to school or a doctor appointment, or it is simply time to eat or go to bed.

A little warning helps the child transition from play to the next activity without feeling disrespected, frustrated, or bossed around. Another way parents might help a child transition into an activity is by purposefully engaging him or her in the process. You might say, "It is dinnertime. I have some potatoes to be washed. Would you like to help me?" You can also get down to the child's eye level, gently touch his or her shoulder, and say, "I see you are having a good time playing, *and* it is now time for us to leave." Again having a consistent daily rhythm and a routine chart smooths transitions and also lessens disruptions of the child's concentration and free play.

Conflicts and Sharing

Conflicts are great opportunities for the child to learn how to communicate his or her needs, be assertive, and develop respectful and healthy social interactions. When helping your child solve a conflict, don't force your child to share, to say "sorry," or express physical affection toward you, a sibling, or a friend. Give him or her the skills she needs.

I might say, "Annabelle, look at Pollyanna and tell her how you feel," or "Pollyanna, tell Annabelle you wish she would stop taking your things." You can use a small toy bug and a wand to help solve your conflicts. You might hold the bug and say, "It *bugs* me when you take my things," and while holding the wand, you say, "I *wish* you would give me space." My children enjoy this sweet technique.

"In time, we will learn to share. Have faith."

Sharing is about learning to give from the heart, respecting the property of others, and developing self-respect. With younger ones, the best approach is always close supervision in order to stop any aggressive nonverbal communication before it happens.

Parents can again walk the child toward a more peaceful and more independent conflict resolution by helping them learn and practice some of the skills they need. Ask your child to look his or her peer or sibling in the eyes and say, "You can have this when I am finished," or "May I please have the ball when you are done?" It is perfectly fine to tell a child, "He is using it now. You may look for something else to do."

Parents of a toddler often want to teach their child to share at the playground or on a playdate. There is social pressure to ensure your young child is sharing. I often ask parents to try to get into the child's world and imagine how the child might be perceiving a situation. I have asked parents to describe how they feel or how they would respond if we role-play some scenarios.

As you read the following questions, take notes on your feelings and decisions. How do you feel when someone takes something of yours without asking? What would you do if someone wanted to use your computer when you were in the middle of writing that important e-mail? What if someone wants to read your novel and takes the book out of your hands? When you are upset because you had your wallet, car, or phone stolen, would you appreciate someone telling you to share?

Often, parents respond with negative feelings and thoughts to those questions. After processing these questions, parents usually perceive the intended meaning of their children's reactions when playing with others. Parents realize that, for young children, being forced to share is unfair and inappropriate, and they start to approach sharing from a different perspective. Sharing becomes a choice, which helps children learn to develop self-confidence and empathy when other children also assert their rights.

After one of my workshops, a mom asked me, *"Can you explain why you said to not force children to apologize? Shouldn't they learn there are some things that are just wrong to do, and you should apologize for them?"* Here's what I told her.

We do want to teach our children that some things are just wrong to do, and they should apologize for those behaviors. However, when we force children to apologize, share, or express affection, we can be taking away the chance to teach them to give or apologize from the heart.

For the young child, *sorry* is just a word. Children quickly learn to use *sorry* as a get-out-of-jail-free pass. They will push and say *sorry* right away so they won't get in trouble. The goal is to prevent children from hurting people's feelings or bodies and to teach empathy. We want the child to actually *feel* sorry and not just to *say sorry*. We also need to respect that the child may not be ready or willing to apologize. Forcing them to do so requires the child to not listen to his or her own feelings and/or to lie about feelings by faking it.

Here are a few ways you can handle apologies:

- Encourage the child to become part of the solution. Invite the child to come up with ways to make up to the other child or to fix the problem he or she created. This action develops feelings of empathy and genuine remorse. Most children come up with much better words and gestures (better than *sorry*) when we ask them, "What can you do to make her feel better?" if the child cannot think of anything to do to repair the situation, you can ask "how about an ice pack?" or "what about if you draw her a picture"
- Use role-play. You can say, "When we hurt others, we can apologize. Would you like to learn how to do it?" Pretend to bump into him or her or mess up his or her play and then apologize. Then have him or her do it to you.
- After a conflict, you can also say, "If you feel badly or sorry, tell me how you feel and I can help you apologize," or "When you are no longer angry, I can help you apologize."
- Genuine apology is best taught through role modeling. Apologize to the child when you are at fault. Make sure you apologize to others in front of him or her. Even make a point of saying how you feel when someone apologizes to you.

Outdoor Play

The land is where our roots are. The children must be taught to feel and live in harmony with the Earth.
—Dr. Maria Montessori

When children are "climbing the walls," we can take away the walls.

Children learn from hands-on, multi sensory experience with the environment, and an important piece is the outdoor environment. The reason why I am including outdoor play here is because our children's outdoor space is one that can also be easily transformed to offer children more sense of purpose.

We fenced or backyard so I would have more peace of mind and would be able to promote more outdoor play for them (specially in the Winter time since I am not good about getting out there with them in the cold weather). I also eliminated the plastic toys, slides or "junkie" gadgets that we had inherited form neighbors and friends. Then replaced those things with a wooden play-house and we outfitted the house with real stainless steel and wooden small dishes and utensils from Good Will.

We added a few garden beds and a compost pile that has allowed us to work and play together in a more purposeful way. We created a wood pile (tree trunks, sticks, and planks that they could use to climb and build with. We also dded a couple of bird feeders, a bunny, and two wooden horses to our backyard.

Now, we start the day outside with our outdoor routine. We bring the compost bin out, we feed the birds, and check on the bunny (clean and feed him). Then we plant, water, weed, or harvest the garden and they play on their mud kitchen or build fairy housed or "forts".

Now, if you don't have a yard or live in a very urban area, you might have to get out of your way to offer opportunities for them to get their hands dirty, gooey, wet and muddy on a daily bases.

One successful way to connect and build a relationship with your child is to go on long walks with him or her. Hike, go to the beach, or walk long distances while quietly contemplating the view.

Research shows that children who play regularly in natural environments show more advanced motor coordination, increased balance and agility, and decreased incidence of sickness. Their activities are more diverse with imaginative, creative play that fosters language and collaborative skills.

My research also shows that exposure to nature improves children's cognitive development by increasing their awareness, reasoning, and observational skills. Nature relieves stress and helps children deal with adversity. Therefore, the greater the amount of exposure to nature, the greater the benefits.

One of the biggest challenge parents reported, when transforming their home environments, was a lack of time to allow their children to do things for themselves when there was so much to do and so many places to be. When families need to leave the house, it is often easier and faster for parents to put children's shoes and jackets on for them than to patiently wait and watch while children struggle to accomplish those tasks on their own.

Parents have shared some solutions for these challenges, which include taking a few extra minutes the night before to set things up and lay things out for the children. Some parents find that waking up a little earlier on school days to allow extra time for the children to dress and get ready without being rushed is worth it. Some figured out they needed to do a lot of preparing with their children the night before. One mom included into their bedtime routine chart picking out clothes, organizing backpacks, and even making lunch. Now her four-year-old daughter helps out with all of those things before bed, and they have smoother mornings.

Transitioning from plastic products to real and breakable child-sized tools and allowing children to independently accomplish daily activities was a little messy at first. It was also a challenge for parents to keep their homes set up and ready for their children. Parents reported having to take a few minutes every day to make sure everything the children need is in place and at their level.

One mom set up a banana-slicing tray or a sandwich-making tray in the evening so they can sleep in a little late on the weekends, as the children can help themselves to breakfast. Another mom put together a couple of cleaning kits with spray bottles, rags, and dustpan and brush at different areas of the home to allow her children to clean up their messes more easily and quickly. One family has eliminated flat sheets from their boys' beds because it is easier for them to make their beds by just straightening the duvet.

Overall, parents have reported great success when they made those simple changes to their home environments. They have reported power struggles, tantrums, and whining lessening, and they have seen improvement in their children's confidence, attention, independence, and organizational skills. Families have seen their children transition from one activity to the next more smoothly. One mom said her boys can now leave their play and happily move into dinnertime mode, as they feel engaged in productive activities such as washing vegetables or setting the table.

Now you have an optimum physical home environment that will promote learning effortlessly throughout the day. Every task is now a learning opportunity for your child. I know that with these simple tools, your child will feel encouraged and empowered to perform everyday tasks independently. Take time to help your child acquire, practice, and master these skills. Set up the environment, and remember not to do for your child what he or she is able to do alone.

All those simple changes to your home will provide your child with that personal power, autonomy, and independence all humans crave. It should also lessen frustration for the children because young children benefit from functioning easily and accomplishing things on their own without feeling frustrated, overwhelmed or overstimulated. At the same time, frustrations are lessened for the adults because we feel we are positively contributing to the child's development. By transferring responsibilities over to the child, we don't need to nag or do all the work ourselves. Most importantly, this more intentional home will show respect, consideration, and appreciation for your child, which helps to build confidence.

Remember that the characteristics and skills we want our children to have as they grow up need to be learned, practiced, and mastered. Children can only learn by watching, doing, and experiencing mistakes. In today's world, children really need the gift of time, our role modeling, and a fair chance to practice those much-needed skills to succeed in life.

Raising a Purposeful Child

Parents can now take a more holistic approach to parenting. We have the opportunity to nurture our children's bodies, minds, and spirits and to give them what no textbook will—the knowledge they have purpose.

No one expects a four-year-old to know calculus. It is understood that a child will learn to rote count, will slowly build upon numerical skills, and will eventually be able to do calculus. Learning is a process—and a very long one. When it comes to social, emotional, and life skills, many parents want immediate change. I encourage parents to delve more deeply into understanding children rather than dismissing their needs and motivations. Often, the way children express and process their emotions can be labeled as poor behavior or one of today's many disorders.

Too often the practice is for parents to dominate the child. However, children behave badly or feel badly about themselves when they perceive adults to be controlling them by giving directives, interfering with their preferred pace of learning, and not allowing them to do things independently. When parents can see their children as merely human beings striving to develop their potential rather than willful children purposely annoying them, parents can learn to approach parenting from an entirely different perspective.

Parenting must begin with recognition, acceptance, and respect for the child as he or she is, rather than from what we think the child should be. A child raised with respect is more likely to engage meaningfully with the environment and others and to feel a better sense of purpose. When we demonstrate faith in him or her and allow that child some freedom of choice, children can start to choose appropriately.

Children need prepared home environments where they can explore, discover, and develop through meaningful, everyday tasks. They also need positive and intentional adults as role models and guides. We must nurture and guide our children, and we must depend on carefully prepared environments as teaching tools. Reducing toys, clutter, and general sensory overload, making the home accessible, establishing rhythms, and adopting a positive approach to discipline are simple ways to protect the grace of childhood in today's fast-paced society.

I always like to close my seminars by reminding parents that change can feel awkward and uncomfortable at first, but eventually all the new parenting concepts and tools become more natural and even second nature. Great parenting is not about perfection but about improvement. The goal is not to raise perfect human beings but to raise people who will do what is right even when we are not watching. Children will do this (be kind, honest, responsible, and more), not for fear of punishment nor for praise or rewards, but simply because it is the right thing to do.

Keep in mind that how we handle everyday parenting challenges will impact what our children will be like as adults. All we do for our children is because we want them to grow to be responsible, kind, resilient, capable, confident, independent, passionate, honest, and creative. We are full of love for them, but it is crucial to our children's development that they see it that way. We must make sure the message of love is getting through in our parenting.

You have received many practical tools to better understand and support your child's development. You can now apply progressive educational principles as well as take a more positive approach to discipline. You have also learned simple strategies for improving important social, emotional, and life skills. Now, with changes in your home environment, you can bring more purpose into your child's life.

I hope this book gave you tools to help your child feel respected, appreciated, and empowered as an important family member. Above all else, I hope these new concepts will guide you to setting the tone for a lifetime of peaceful and positive interaction between you and your child.

Don't forget. When in doubt, fall back on love.

About the Author

Lorena Seidel is a Montessori teacher, a social-emotional consultant, and a mother of three. She helps teachers and parents build a more peaceful, positive and purposeful relationship with children. This is accomplished through providing children the optimum learning environment - both physically (home/school) and emotionally (climate set by the adults). Lorena is a certified Montessori teacher by the American Montessori Society(AMS) and has taught for many years at the Whitby School, located in Greenwich, CT. Lorena is a trained Positive Discipline Parent and Teacher Educator and has helped thousands of teachers and parents through coaching, workshops, lectures, parent-child classes, and school consulting. Lorena's goal is to help children develop valuable academic, social-emotional, and life skills using everyday life as opportunities to teach and learn. With Lorena's help parents and teachers are bring up more independent, resilient, responsible, capable, and emotionally stable children. Lorena has received a Bachelor of Arts Degree in Education and Linguistics from the Pontificate Catholic University in Brazil and a degree in Literature from the University of Connecticut. Lorena has a Master of Arts of Elementary Education from Sacred Heart University, and she is also an International Baccalaureate Organization (IBO) trained teacher. Lorena is the founder of The Purposeful Child and has authored interactive parenting e-book "Everyday Montessori" and "The Purposeful Child" DVD series. Lorena lives in Connecticut with her husband Andrew and her sweet daughters Pollyanna, Annabelle, and Julliette.

References

Adler, A. *Understanding Human Nature*. Eastford, CT: Martino Publishing, 2010.

Chang, M., B. Park, and S. Kim. "Parenting Classes, Parenting Behavior, and Child Cognitive Development in Early Head Start: A Longitudinal Model." *School Community Journal* 20 (2009): 155–74.

Cooke, N., A. G. Kretlow, and S. Helf. "Supplemental Reading Help for Kindergarten Students: How Early Should You Start?" *Journal Articles Reports* 8 (2010): 137–44.

Cossentino, J. "Following All the Children: Early Intervention and Montessori." *Montessori Life: A Publication of the American Montessori Society* 8 (2010): 38–45.

Dreikurs, R. *Children: The Challenge*. New York: Hawthorn Books, 1964.

Edwards, C. P. "Three Approaches from Europe: Waldorf, Montessori, and Reggio Emilia." (2002).

Faber, A., and E. Mazlish. *How to Talk So Kids Will Listen and Listen So Kids Will Talk*. New York–London: W. W. Norton & Company, 1987.

Faber, A., and E. Mazlish. *Siblings Without Rivalry: How to Help Your Children Live So You Can Live Too*. New York–London: W. W. Norton & Company, 1987.

Ginott, H. *Between Parent and Child*. New York: Three Rivers Press, 1965.

Gilder, S. A. "Hands as Companions of the Mind: Essential Practical Life for the Five-Year-Old." *Montessori Life: A Publication of the American Montessori Society* 6 (2012): 24–29.

Haskins, C. "Order, Organization, and Beauty in the Classroom: A Prerequisite, Not an Option." *Montessori Life: A Publication of the American Montessori Society* 6 (2012): 34–39.

Haskins, C. "The Gift of Silence." *Montessori Life: A Publication of the American Montessori Society* 6 (2011): 34–39.

Kayili, G., and R. Ari. "Examination of the Effects of the Montessori Method on Preschool Children's Readiness to Primary Education." *Educational Sciences: Theory and Practice* 6 (2011): 2104–09.

Lillard, A. "How Important Are the Montessori Materials?" *Montessori Life: A Publication of the American Montessori Society* 6 (2008): 20–25.

Lillard, A. *Montessori: The Science Behind the Genius*. Oxford: Oxford University Press, 2008.

Medina, J. *Brain Rules: 12 Principles for Surviving and Thriving at Work, Home, and School.* Seattle: Pear Press, 2010.

Montessori, M. *The Absorbent Mind.* New York: Holt, Rinehart and Winston, 1967.

Montessori, M. *The Montessori Method.* New York: Schocken Books, 1964.

Murray, A. "Montessori Elementary Philosophy Reflects Current Motivation Theories." *Montessori Life: A Publication of the American Montessori Society* 12 (2012): 22–33.

Nelsen, J. *Positive Discipline: The Classic Guide to Helping Children Develop Self-Discipline, Responsibility, Cooperation and Problem-Solving Skills.* New York: Ballantine Books, 2006.

Payne, K. J., and L. Ross. *Simplicity Parenting: Using the Extraordinary Power of Less to Raise Calmer, Happier, and More Secure Kids.* New York: Ballantine Books, 2010. Peters, D. L. "The Child Whisperer." *Montessori Life: A Publication of the American Montessori Society* 3 (2012): 24–26.

Santos, R., A. Fettig, and L. Shaffer. "Helping Families Connect Early Literacy with Social-Emotional Development." *Young Children* 6 (2012): 88–93.

Saracho, O. N., and B. Spodek. "Educating the Young Mathematician: The Twentieth Century and Beyond." *Early Childhood Education Journal* 8 (2009): 305–12.

Seldin, T. *How to Raise an Amazing Child the Montessori Way.* New York: DK Publishing, 2006.

Stephenson, S. M. *The Joyful Child: Michael Olaf's Essential Montessori for Birth to Three.* Arcata, CA: Michael Olaf Montessori Company, 2006.

Thayer-Bacon, B. "Montessori, John Dewey, and William H. Kilpatrick." *Education and Culture* 18 (2012): 3–20.

Thomason, A., and K. La Paro. "Early Education and Development." *Taylor & Francis Group* 20, no. 2 (2009): 285–304.

Weinberg, D. "Maria Montessori and the Secret of Tabula Rasa." *Montessori Life: A Publication of the American Montessori Society* 6 (2009): 30–35.

Weinberg, D. R. "Montessori, Maslow, and Self-Actualization." *Montessori Life: A Publication of the American Montessori Society* 6 (2012): 16–21.

CPSIA information can be obtained
at www.ICGtesting.com
Printed in the USA
LVOW05s1135101215

466141LV00022B/64/P

9 781480 815636